Reading and Note Taking Study Guide

MAGRUDER'S
AMERICAN
GOVERNMENT

PEARSON

Boston, Massachusetts • Chandler, Arizona • Glenview, Illinois • New York, New York

Acknowledgments

Grateful acknowledgment is made to the following for copyrighted material:

Images:
Cover: Comstock/Stockbyte/Getty Images; Ruaridh Stewart/ZUMA/Corbis (Ronald Reagan button)

ISBN-13:   978-0-32-888037-9

ISBN-10:   0-32-888037-X

5   17

Contents
Magruder's American Government
Reading and Note Taking Study Guide

How to use the *Reading and Note Taking Study Guide*

The **Reading and Note Taking Study Guide** will help you better understand the content of *Magruder's American Government*. It will also help you develop your note taking, reading, and vocabulary skills. Each study guide consists of three components. The first component focuses on developing a graphic organizer for the material covered by each topic that will help you take notes as you read.

Name _____ Class _____ Date _____

TOPIC 7
Note Taking Study Guide
THE JUDICIAL BRANCH

Focus Question: How should we handle conflict?

As you read, note the various courts of the U.S. federal judicial system—the branch of government that handles legal conflict.

The Judicial Branch of the Federal Government

COURTS	POWERS, JURISDICTION
Constitutional Courts	• deal with matters involving the "judicial power of the United States" •
Supreme Court	• • •
Courts of appeals	• • do not conduct trials or accept new evidence •
District courts	• conduct federal trials in a total of 94 courts, at least one per State •
Court of International Trade	•
Special Courts	•
Court of Appeals for the Armed Forces	• can review the more serious court-martial convictions of military personnel •
Court of Appeals for Veterans Claims	• • decides appeals regarding veterans' benefits
Court of Federal Claims	•
Tax Court	•
Territorial courts	•

63

The **Focus Question** gives you a tool to focus your reading.

Each **Note Taking Study Guide** has one graphic organizer for every topic. Completing the graphic organizer will help you comprehend the material and retain important details. Use your completed graphic organizer to review and prepare for assessments.

The second component highlights the central themes, issues, and concepts of each lesson in the topic.

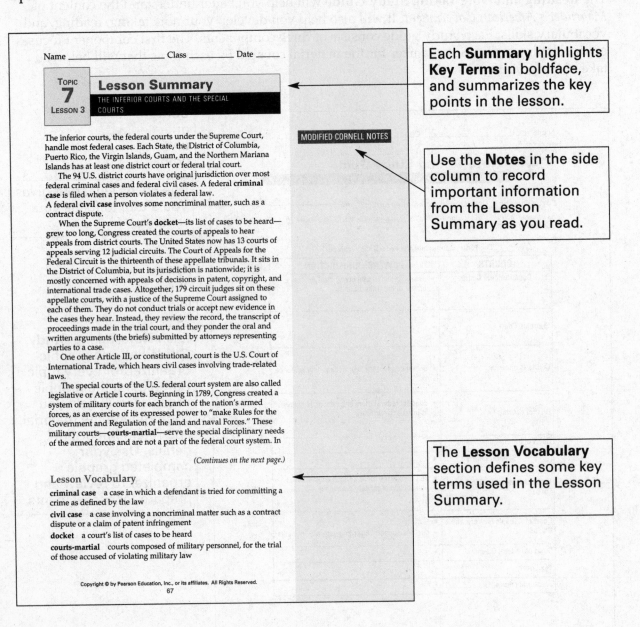

Name _____ Class _____ Date _____

TOPIC
7
LESSON 3

Lesson Summary
THE INFERIOR COURTS AND THE SPECIAL COURTS

The inferior courts, the federal courts under the Supreme Court, handle most federal cases. Each State, the District of Columbia, Puerto Rico, the Virgin Islands, Guam, and the Northern Mariana Islands has at least one district court or federal trial court.

The 94 U.S. district courts have original jurisdiction over most federal criminal cases and federal civil cases. A federal **criminal case** is filed when a person violates a federal law.

A federal **civil case** involves some noncriminal matter, such as a contract dispute.

When the Supreme Court's **docket**—its list of cases to be heard—grew too long, Congress created the courts of appeals to hear appeals from district courts. The United States now has 13 courts of appeals serving 12 judicial circuits. The Court of Appeals for the Federal Circuit is the thirteenth of these appellate tribunals. It sits in the District of Columbia, but its jurisdiction is nationwide; it is mostly concerned with appeals of decisions in patent, copyright, and international trade cases. Altogether, 179 circuit judges sit on these appellate courts, with a justice of the Supreme Court assigned to each of them. They do not conduct trials or accept new evidence in the cases they hear. Instead, they review the record, the transcript of proceedings made in the trial court, and they ponder the oral and written arguments (the briefs) submitted by attorneys representing parties to a case.

One other Article III, or constitutional, court is the U.S. Court of International Trade, which hears civil cases involving trade-related laws.

The special courts of the U.S. federal court system are also called legislative or Article I courts. Beginning in 1789, Congress created a system of military courts for each branch of the nation's armed forces, as an exercise of its expressed power to "make Rules for the Government and Regulation of the land and naval Forces." These military courts—**courts-martial**—serve the special disciplinary needs of the armed forces and are not a part of the federal court system. In

(Continues on the next page.)

Lesson Vocabulary

criminal case a case in which a defendant is tried for committing a crime as defined by the law

civil case a case involving a noncriminal matter such as a contract dispute or a claim of patent infringement

docket a court's list of cases to be heard

courts-martial courts composed of military personnel, for the trial of those accused of violating military law

MODIFIED CORNELL NOTES

Each **Summary** highlights **Key Terms** in boldface, and summarizes the key points in the lesson.

Use the **Notes** in the side column to record important information from the Lesson Summary as you read.

The **Lesson Vocabulary** section defines some key terms used in the Lesson Summary.

The third component consists of review questions that assess your understanding of each lesson in the topic.

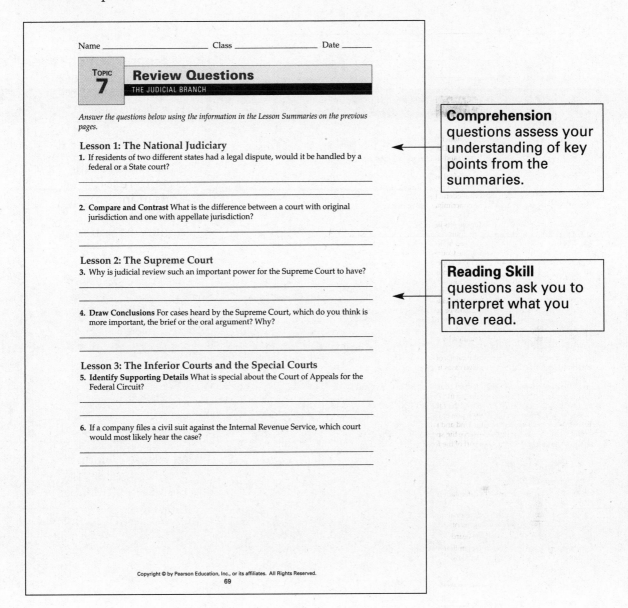

Name _____ Class _____ Date _____

Answer the questions below using the information in the Lesson Summaries on the previous pages.

Lesson 1: The National Judiciary

1. If residents of two different states had a legal dispute, would it be handled by a federal or a State court?

_____

2. **Compare and Contrast** What is the difference between a court with original jurisdiction and one with appellate jurisdiction?

_____

Lesson 2: The Supreme Court

3. Why is judicial review such an important power for the Supreme Court to have?

_____

4. **Draw Conclusions** For cases heard by the Supreme Court, which do you think is more important, the brief or the oral argument? Why?

_____

Lesson 3: The Inferior Courts and the Special Courts

5. **Identify Supporting Details** What is special about the Court of Appeals for the Federal Circuit?

_____

6. If a company files a civil suit against the Internal Revenue Service, which court would most likely hear the case?

_____

Comprehension questions assess your understanding of key points from the summaries.

Reading Skill questions ask you to interpret what you have read.

TOPIC 1

Note Taking Study Guide

FOUNDATIONS OF GOVERNMENT

Focus Question: What should government do?

As you read, note how various forms of government distribute or concentrate power in order to accomplish governmental functions.

Form of Government	Distribution or Concentration of Power
dictatorship	
	Supreme political power rests with the people; the majority rules, but minority rights are respected.
autocracy	
	A small elite holds the power to rule.
unitary	
federal	
presidential	
	Power is focused on the legislative branch, which elects the executive branch.
republic	
monarchy	

TOPIC **1** LESSON 1	**Lesson Summary**
	PRINCIPLES OF GOVERNMENT

MODIFIED CORNELL NOTES

Government is the institution through which a society makes and enforces its **public policies**—all the things a government decides to do. Every government has three kinds of power: **legislative power**, or the power to establish law; **executive power**, or the power to carry out the law; and **judicial power**, or the power to interpret laws and settle disputes. These powers are often outlined in a **constitution**—the body of laws that sets out a government's structure, principles, and processes.

In a **dictatorship**, one person or a small group may exercise all the powers of government. In a **democracy**, supreme authority over government rests with the people.

The world's dominant political unit is the **state**—a body of people living in a defined territory, often called a nation or country. Every state has four characteristics: **population**; **territory** or land; **sovereignty** or absolute power; and government.

(Continues on the next page.)

Lesson Vocabulary

government the institution through which a society makes and enforces its public policies

public policies all of the things a government decides to do

legislative power the power to make laws and to frame public policies

executive power the power to execute, enforce, and administer laws

judicial power the power to interpret laws, to determine their meaning, and to settle disputes that arise within the society

constitution the body of fundamental laws setting out the principles, structures, and processes of a government

dictatorship form of government where those who rule cannot be held responsible to the will of the people

democracy form of government where supreme authority rests with the people

state a body of people, living in a defined territory, organized politically (that is, with a government), and with the power to make and enforce law without the consent of any higher authority

population the number of people in a particular state or other area

territory the land, with known and recognized boundaries, claimed by a state

sovereignty a state's supreme and absolute power within its own territory

Lesson Summary
PRINCIPLES OF GOVERNMENT (continued)

There are four theories for the origin of the state. The **force theory** says that one person or a small group claimed control over an area and forced all within it to submit to that person's or group's rule. According to those that believe the **evolutionary theory**, the state developed naturally out of the early family of which one person was the leader and therefore the "government." The **theory of the divine right of kings** held that God created the state and that God had given those of royal birth a "divine right" to rule. According to the **social contract theory**, people gave up to the state some freedoms in order to promote the safety and well-being of all, and the state created a government to exercise the powers given to it.

The Preamble to the U.S. Constitution describes the goals of the United States Federal Government. It says that government should form a more perfect union, or keep the States working together; establish justice; ensure domestic tranquility, or keep order; provide for the common defense; promote the general welfare; and secure the blessings of liberty.

Lesson Vocabulary

force theory   the idea that the state was born when one individual or group claimed control of an area and forced others within it to submit to that person's or group's rule

evolutionary theory   the idea that the state arose out of the early family, which over time developed into a network of families and then into a tribe and, with the rise of agriculture, into a state

theory of the divine right of kings   the idea that God grants authority to a government

social contract theory   the idea that people, who had freedom but lacked protection and security, agreed with one another to create a state in which they would, through a social contract, give up as much power to the state as needed to promote the safety and well-being of all

Name _____ Class _____ Date _____

Lesson Summary
TYPES OF GOVERNMENT

MODIFIED CORNELL NOTES

Governments may be classified in three ways. The first is defined by who may participate in the government. In a democracy, supreme political authority rests with the people. An indirect democracy is a representative democracy in which a small group of people are chosen to represent the people. Some people insist that the United States is more properly called a republic rather than a democracy because in a republic the sovereign power is held by those eligible to vote, while the political power is exercised by representatives.

All dictatorships are authoritarian, meaning that the ruler holds absolute authority over the people. A dictatorship may be totalitarian, meaning that the rulers control nearly every aspect of human affairs. It may also be an **autocracy**, in which one person holds unlimited political power; or an **oligarchy**, in which a small elite holds the power to rule; or a **theocracy**, in which the legal system is based on religious law.

The second classification is defined by where government power is held. In a **unitary government**, a single, central agency holds all governmental powers. In a **federal government**, a central government and several local governments share governmental powers in a division of powers. Because the Constitution divides power between the National Government and the States, the United States is a federal government. A federal system is different from a **confederation**, which is an alliance of independent states.

The third type of classification describes the relationship between the legislative and the executive branches of government. A **presidential government** divides power between the branches, while a **parliamentary government** focuses power on the legislative branch. In the latter, the executive branch is chosen by and subject to the legislative branch.

Lesson Vocabulary

autocracy a form of government in which a single person holds unlimited power

oligarchy a form of government in which the power to rule is held by a small, usually self-appointed elite

theocracy a form of government in which the legal system is based on religious law

unitary government a centralized government in which all government powers belong to a single, central agency

federal government a form of government in which powers are divided between a central government and several local governments

confederation a joining of several groups for a common purpose

presidential government a form of government in which the executive and legislative branches of the government are separate, independent, and coequal

parliamentary government a form of government in which the executive branch is made up of the prime minister, or premier, and that official's cabinet; this branch is part of the legislature

Lesson Summary
ORIGINS OF THE MODERN DEMOCRATIC STATE

MODIFIED CORNELL NOTES

The roots of democratic government reach back to ancient Greece and Rome and include elements related to Judeo-Christian philosophy. The concept of democracy was born in Athens, Greece in 700–800 *b.c.* At about the same time, the Romans developed a form of government which they referred to as a republic. The Romans held elections to choose some public officials, thus introducing the concept of representation.

The decline and fall of the Roman Empire marked the collapse of organized government over much of the Western world. The feudal system was born in response to the resulting disorder. **Feudalism** was a loosely organized system in which powerful lords divided their land among other, lesser lords.

At the end of the Middle Ages, a commercial revolution began to change the ways in which people lived and did business. The economy became increasingly based on money and trade, rather than land. Towns began to spring up across Europe, and those towns tested the limits of feudalism. The monarchs saw the towns as a source of wealth. By the late 1400s, the powers of the monarchs were expanding, and feudalism was fast disappearing.

Monarchs, whose power was absolute or nearly so, had **sovereignty**, or the highest authority in decision making and in maintaining order. However, claiming sovereignty alone does not establish government. All governments must have legitimacy to rule. **Legitimacy** is the belief of the people that a government has the right to make public policy. Governments may gain legitimacy in several ways. One way is known as the **divine right of kings**, the belief that God granted monarchs the right to rule. Another way to win legitimacy is through the power of personality. The final and most durable form of legitimacy is created when a government binds itself to the rule of law.

(Continues on the next page.)

Lesson Vocabulary

feudalism a loosely organized system in which powerful lords divided their land among other, lesser lords

sovereignty utmost authority in decision making and in maintaining order of a state

legitimacy the belief of the people that a government has the right to make public policy

divine right of kings the belief that God grants authority to a government

TOPIC 1 — LESSON 3

Lesson Summary

ORIGINS OF THE MODERN DEMOCRATIC STATE (continued)

MODIFIED CORNELL NOTES

Colonialism is the control of one nation over lands abroad. Colonial trade brought power to merchants, and monarchs adopted mercantilism to control and profit from that situation. **Mercantilism** is an economic and political theory emphasizing money as the chief source of wealth to increase the absolute power of the monarchy and the nation.

Some of the most important ideas about modern government, economics, and society were developed during the Enlightenment. John Locke introduced the idea of the natural rights of all human beings. Thomas Hobbes believed that the people and their rulers are parties to a social contract that defines the rights and powers of each. Adam Smith and David Ricardo criticized policies that had helped monarchs grow wealthier while most of their subjects became poorer. François-Marie Arouet (known as Voltaire) advocated reason, freedom of religion, the importance of scientific observation, and the idea of human progress. Baron de Montesquieu developed theories about the separation of the powers of government. William Blackstone believed in the idea that legal decisions should be made on the basis of similar decisions made in the past.

Lesson Vocabulary

colonialism   the control of one nation over foreign lands

mercantilism   an economic and political theory emphasizing money as the chief source of wealth to increase the absolute power of the monarchy and the nation

TOPIC 1 — LESSON 4

Lesson Summary
THE BASICS OF DEMOCRACY

The American concept of democracy rests on five basic notions. First, each individual has worth. Second, all individuals are equal. Third, the majority of the people rules, but the majority must respect the rights of any minority. Fourth, **compromise**, or the blending and adjusting of competing interests, is necessary. Fifth, each individual must have the widest possible degree of freedom.

Citizenship in this country has both duties and responsibilities. The duties all revolve around a citizen's commitment to obey the law. Responsibilities all come down to an abiding respect for each of the core beliefs on which democracy is based.

The American commitment to freedom is evident in the nation's economic system. This system, often called the **free enterprise system**, is based on private ownership, individual initiative, profit, and competition. Also known as capitalism, this system does not rely on the government to make economic decisions. Rather, individuals make those decisions based on the law of supply and demand. The law of supply and demand states that when supplies of goods and services become plentiful, prices tend to drop; when supplies become scarcer, prices tend to rise.

Lesson Vocabulary

compromise an adjustment of opposing principles or systems by modifying some aspect of each in order to find the position most acceptable to the majority

free enterprise system an economic system characterized by private or corporate ownership of capital goods; investments that are determined by private decision rather than by state control and determined in a free market

TOPIC 1	**Review Questions**
	FOUNDATIONS OF GOVERNMENT

Answer the questions below using the information in the Lesson Summaries on the previous pages.

Lesson 1: Principles of Government

1. Compare and Contrast How is a government conducted under a dictatorship? How does a dictatorship differ from a democracy?

_____

_____

2. What are the three basic kinds of power that all governments have?

_____

_____

Lesson 2: Types of Government

3. Identify Supporting Details Adolf Hitler is usually referred to as a dictator. Under what circumstances would it also be accurate to call him an autocrat?

_____

_____

4. In a federal system of government, what governments share power?

_____

_____

Lesson 3: Origins of the Modern Democratic State

5. Why do discussions of the origin of democratic government often look back at Greece and Rome?

_____

_____

6. Draw Conclusions Can a government ruled by a monarch have legitimacy? Why or why not?

_____

_____

Lesson 4: The Basics of Democracy

7. Draw Inferences Three of the five basic notions on which democracy is based have to do with individuals. How might those ideas clash with another basic notion, that of compromise?

_____

_____

8. Compare and Contrast How does the American free enterprise economic system reflect the respect for the individual that is basic to the American political system?

_____

_____

TOPIC 2

Note Taking Study Guide
THE BEGINNINGS OF AMERICAN GOVERNMENT

Focus Question: How much power should a government have?

As you read, note how the American colonists and, later, the citizens of the newly independent United States dealt with the issue of how much power a government should have.

English Colonists' Key Ideas about Government
• ordered government
•
•

Government Under the Articles of Confederation
• lacked power to tax
•
•

Issues Related to Government Power

First Continental Congress
•

• trade regulations

Constitutional Convention
• sharing of central government's power among three branches
•

TOPIC 2 LESSON 1
Lesson Summary
ORIGINS OF AMERICAN POLITICAL IDEALS

The colonists brought with them to North America knowledge of the English political system, including three key ideas about government. The first idea was that of **ordered government**. This means that a government's rules should help people get along. The second idea of **limited government** means that government has restricted powers. The third idea of **representative government** means that government should serve the people.

The English tradition of government grew from three landmark documents. The Magna Carta (1215) states that the king does not have total power. It also protects the rights of trial by jury and **due process** of law. The Petition of Right (1628) states that the king cannot use the military to rule during peacetime or let soldiers live in people's homes. The English Bill of Rights (1689) forbids keeping an army during peacetime, guarantees a fair and speedy trial, and ensures that all parliamentary elections are free.

The three types of English colonies each provided training for the colonists in the art of government. Each colony was based on a **charter**, a written grant of authority from the king. Royal colonies were ruled directly by the Crown. **Proprietary** colonies were organized by a proprietor, or owner, who was granted land by the king. Charter colonies were based on charters granted directly to the colonists. Most colonies had **bicameral** (two-house) legislatures, although Pennsylvania's was **unicameral** (one-house).

Lesson Vocabulary

ordered government   a system that provides orderly regulation of citizens' relationships with one another

limited government   basic principle of American government, which states that government is restricted in what it may do, and each individual has rights that government cannot take away; *see* constitutionalism, popular sovereignty

representative government   system of government in which public policies are made by officials selected by the voters and held accountable in periodic elections; *see* democracy

due process   doctrine that holds that the government must act fairly and in accord with established rules in all that it does

charter   a city's basic law, its constitution; a written grant of authority from the king

proprietary   organized by a proprietor (a person to whom the king had made a grant of land)

bicameral   an adjective describing a legislative body composed of two chambers

unicameral   an adjective describing a legislative body with one chamber; *see* bicameral

TOPIC 2 LESSON 2
Lesson Summary
INDEPENDENCE

Great Britain became more involved in ruling its colonies in the 1760s. It created new taxes and laws that caused the colonists to object to "taxation without representation."

The colonists reacted to the changes in British policy by taking small steps toward unity. The New England States had already formed a **confederation**, or union for a common purpose, in the 1600s. In 1754, Benjamin Franklin's Albany Plan of Union proposed a congress of **delegates**, or representatives, from all colonies. The congress would have had the power to raise a military, negotiate with the Native Americans, and collect customs **duties**, but both the colonies and the king rejected it.

Twelve of the thirteen colonies joined at the First Continental Congress in 1774. They met to plan opposition to harsh British policies and punishment of colonists who resisted. The delegates sent a Declaration of Rights, protesting Britain's colonial policies, to King George III and urged the colonies to refuse all trade with England until the hated taxes and trade regulations were repealed. The delegates also made plans to meet again.

Finally, the colonists were ready to fight. The American Revolution began on April 19, 1775. On May 10, 1775, the Second Continental Congress began. It became the first government of the new United States and produced the Declaration of Independence.

The Declaration of Independence was largely the work of Thomas Jefferson. He based much of his writing on the social contract theory, which asserted that people have the right to form governments to protect their natural rights. After much debate, the delegates adopted the Declaration of Independence on July 4, 1776.

The newly formed States wrote constitutions. A constitution is the basic set of laws that creates a government. The State constitutions all shared the principle of **popular sovereignty**, meaning that government can exist only with the consent of the people governed. They also shared a commitment to limited government, civil rights and liberties, and a separation of powers.

Lesson Vocabulary

confederation   the joining of several groups for a common purpose

delegates   people with authority to represent others at a conference or convention

duties taxes levied on imports

popular sovereignty   the idea that government can exist only with the consent of the people governed

Name _____ Class _____ Date _____

MODIFIED CORNELL NOTES

The 1780s were problem-filled years for the United States. Although the States wanted a permanent government, they did not want to give it much power.

The Articles of Confederation received the formal approval, or **ratification**, of the thirteen States in 1781. The Articles set up a government that tied the States together in a loose union. This government consisted of only one branch, the Congress, which was unicameral. Each State had one vote. Each year, Congress was to choose one of its members as its presiding officer. Congress had the power to set up an army and a navy, make war and peace, and settle State disputes. The States promised to provide the funds and troops requested by Congress; treat citizens of other States fairly and equally within their own borders; and give **full faith and credit** to the public acts, records, and judicial proceedings of every other State. The limited powers granted to Congress soon proved to be problematic. The National Government did not have the power to tax, regulate trade, or force the States to obey the Articles or the laws passed by the legislature.

With a central government unable to act, the States were soon arguing, taxing one another, and printing their own money. Economic chaos followed and led to violence, the worst of which occurred in a series of incidents in Massachusetts that came to be known as Shays' Rebellion.

Many leaders were convinced that Americans had to strengthen the government. Delegates from Maryland and Virginia met at Mount Vernon, Virginia, to solve their trade problems. Their success led them to call a meeting at Annapolis, Maryland, to try to solve some of the nation's problems. Only five States sent delegates. They set up another meeting in Philadelphia, Pennsylvania, which became the Constitutional Convention.

Lesson Vocabulary

ratification   formal approval or final consent to the effectiveness of a constitution, constitutional amendment, or treaty

full faith and credit   clause requiring that each State accept the public acts, records, and judicial proceedings of every other State

TOPIC 2 LESSON 4

Lesson Summary
CREATING AND RATIFYING THE CONSTITUTION

In 1787, fifty-five delegates from twelve States met in Philadelphia to revise the Articles of Confederation. Later known as the Framers, these delegates soon decided to write a new constitution instead.

With a **quorum**, or majority, of States represented, the delegates started the meeting and unanimously elected George Washington president of the convention. They then set about writing a new constitution.

The delegates from Virginia were the first to offer a plan. The Virginia Plan called for three branches of government: executive, legislative, and judicial. The number of representatives a State sent to the bicameral legislature was linked to its wealth and population. Two branches of the new government—the executive and the judicial—could **veto**, or reject, acts passed by Congress, but the two houses of the legislature could override a veto. Small States opposed this plan. The New Jersey Plan called for a government without strong and separate branches. It also proposed a unicameral legislature with an equal number of representatives from each State.

The Constitution became a document of compromises. The Connecticut Compromise combined the basic features of the Virginia and New Jersey plans. It called for two houses in Congress. In the smaller Senate, the States would have equal representation. In the larger House, each State would be represented based on its population. The Three-Fifths Compromise determined that States could count three-fifths of their slaves as part of their populations, which increased their representation in the House. The Commerce and Slave Trade Compromise forbade Congress from taxing exports from any State as well as from acting against the slave trade for twenty years. The Framers made many other compromises before they completed their work on September 17, 1787.

The Framers had provided that before the Constitution could take effect, at least nine of the thirteen States had to ratify it. Americans were greatly divided in their opinions about the Constitution. Two groups formed during the ratification process: the Federalists, who favored ratifying the Constitution, and the Anti-Federalists, who strongly opposed it. The Federalists stressed the weaknesses of the Articles of Confederation. Anti-Federalists attacked almost every part of the Constitution, but one of its features drew the strongest criticism: the lack of a bill of rights that would provide for basic liberties such as freedom of speech and religion.

(Continues on the next page.)

Lesson Vocabulary

quorum   fewest number of members who must be present for a legislative body to conduct business; majority

veto   chief executive's power to reject a bill passed by a legislature; literally (Latin) "I forbid"

TOPIC 2 LESSON 4

Lesson Summary

CREATING AND RATIFYING THE CONSTITUTION (continued)

Over the course of the struggle for ratification, an extraordinary number of essays, speeches, letters, and other commentaries were printed. Ratification happened fairly quickly in nine States, but the struggle for ratification was intense in Virginia and New York, both of which were critical to the success of the new government. Thanks to the support of Thomas Jefferson in Virginia and Alexander Hamilton in New York, the Federalists finally won in both States.

After eleven States ratified the Constitution in 1788, the States held elections for a new President. The first Congress of the new National Government met in March 1789. Because there was not a quorum, the electoral votes could not be counted until April 6. At that point, the first Congress declared George Washington President of the United States.

Name _____ Class _____ Date _____

Answer the questions below using the information in the Lesson Summaries on the previous pages.

Lesson 1: Origins of American Political Ideals

1. What were three basic concepts that English colonists brought with them to America?

_____

2. **Compare and Contrast** How do the Petition of Right and the English Bill of Rights differ in regard to the military?

_____

_____

Lesson 2: Independence

3. **Assess an Argument** The colonists objected to "taxation without representation." What kind of taxation do you think they would have supported? Why?

_____

_____

4. Who was the main author of the Declaration of Independence?

_____

_____

Lesson 3: First Steps

5. Describe the structure of the central government under the Articles of Confederation.

_____

_____

6. **Identify Causes and Effects** What were the main effects of having a weak central government under the Articles of Confederation?

_____

_____

Lesson 4: Creating and Ratifying the Constitution

7. **Draw Inferences** How were the Senate and the House structured as a result of the Connecticut Compromise? Why was that compromise so important?

_____

_____

8. **Compare and Contrast** How did the Federalists differ from the Anti-Federalists on the issue of the central government's power and the ratification of the Constitution?

_____

_____

TOPIC 3

Note Taking Study Guide

THE CONSTITUTION

Focus Question: What is the right balance of power in good government?

As you read, note instances in which a balance of power is sought within and among governments.

Principle or Concept	How a Balance of Power Is Sought
bicameralism	
	The government possesses only the power that the people give it.
separation of powers	
	Each branch of the central government has ways to limit the power of the other two branches.
federalism	
amendments	
Full Faith and Credit Clause	

MODIFIED CORNELL NOTES

The Constitution sets out the basic principles upon which government in the United States was built and operates today. It originally consisted of a Preamble, or introduction, and seven sections called articles. The first three articles deal with the three branches of the National Government: Congress, the presidency, and the federal court system.

Article I establishes a **bicameral** legislature, that is, a legislature made up of two houses. This system reflects the British system of bicameralism, and the type of government found in eleven of the thirteen States. This bicameral system met the need for a federalist government. Finally, bicameralism was a way to diffuse the power of Congress and prevent it from overwhelming the other two branches of government.

Article II of the Constitution is known as the Executive Article. It established the presidency.

Article III established both the national judicial system and the State court system. It gave Congress the ability to create **inferior courts**, or the lower federal courts that are beneath the Supreme Court. There are two types of federal courts: the constitutional courts and the special courts. The constitutional courts are also known as the regular courts, or Article III courts. The special courts are known as the Article I courts, which hear a narrower range of cases.

The Framers developed the Preamble and all seven articles around the six broad ideas, or principles, described below:

- **Popular sovereignty** is the idea that the people are the source of all power held by the government.
- **Limited government** means that the government possesses only the powers the people give it—it must obey the Constitution. This principle is also known as **constitutionalism**. Government officials are subject to the **rule of law**—they must always obey the law and are never above it.
- **Separation of powers** establishes three separate parts, or branches, that share the government's power. These branches are the executive, the legislative, and the judicial.

(Continues on the next page.)

Lesson Vocabulary

bicameral   having two parts; describing a legislative body composed of two chambers

inferior courts   the lower federal courts, under the Supreme Court

Name _____ Class _____ Date _____

TOPIC 3 LESSON 1

Lesson Summary
AN OVERVIEW OF THE CONSTITUTION (continued)

MODIFIED CORNELL NOTES

- The Constitution uses a system of **checks and balances** to ensure that none of the three branches can become too powerful. Each branch has ways to limit the power of the other two. An example of this principle is the power of the President to veto, or reject, any act of Congress. Congress may then override a veto with a two-thirds vote in each house.
- **Judicial review**, the fifth principle, is the power of the courts to decide what the Constitution means. The courts also have the power to declare a government action to be against the Constitution, or **unconstitutional**.
- Lastly, the Framers used the principle of **federalism** to divide power between the central government and the States.

Lesson Vocabulary

checks and balances   system of overlapping the powers of the legislative, executive, and judicial branches to permit each branch to check the actions of the others

judicial review the power of courts to decide what the Constitution means

unconstitutional   contrary to constitutional provision and so illegal, null and void, of no force and effect

federalism   a system of government in which a written constitution divides power between a central, or national, government and several regional governments like States

TOPIC 3 LESSON 2 — Lesson Summary

AMENDING THE CONSTITUTION

The Constitution has lasted more than 200 years because it has changed with the times. Many of its words and their meanings are the same, but some words have been changed, eliminated, or added; some of the word meanings have changed over time as well. The alterations to the Constitution have occurred in two ways: either through formal or informal **amendments**, or changes.

A **formal amendment** is a change to the Constitution's written words. The Framers created four ways to make such changes. The Framers followed the principle of federalism in creating these methods. First, amendments are proposed, or suggested, at a national level—either by Congress or at a national convention. Then they are ratified at the State level—either in the State legislatures or by State conventions. This first method has been used for all but one of the 27 amendments.

Note that the formal amendment process emphasizes the federal character of the governmental system. Proposal takes place at the national level and ratification is a State-by-State matter.

If a State rejects a proposed amendment, it is not forever bound by that action. It may later reconsider and ratify the proposal. Ratification must take place within "a reasonable time limit," usually seven years.

The first 10 amendments are the Bill of Rights. Congress proposed all of them in 1789 because many people refused to support the Constitution unless the Federal Government protected these basic rights. The States approved these 10 amendments in 1791. The other 17 amendments became part of the Constitution one at a time.

Many informal changes to the Constitution have been made since 1787. Unlike formal amendments, these changes have not altered the Constitution's actual words. These changes have come from five sources:

- Congress has made changes to the Constitution through two kinds of basic legislation. First, it has passed thousands of laws that explain certain parts of the Constitution. Second, it has passed laws that fill in details about the specific ways the government operates.

(Continues on the next page.)

Lesson Vocabulary

amendment   a change in or addition to a constitution or law

formal amendment   change or addition that becomes part of the written language of the Constitution itself through one of four methods set forth in the Constitution

MODIFIED CORNELL NOTES

- The way Presidents have used their powers has produced some informal changes. For example, a President may choose to make an **executive agreement**, or pact, with the head of another country instead of a **treaty**, or formal agreement, between two sovereign countries that requires congressional approval.

- The courts, especially the U.S. Supreme Court, have informally changed the Constitution by explaining parts of it when ruling on cases. They also decide if government actions are constitutional.

- Political parties have informally shaped what the government does. For example, the parties have decreased the importance of the **electoral college**, the group that formally selects the nation's President.

- Customs are the usual ways people do things. Many customs have developed in American government that are not mentioned in the Constitution. For example, the President's Cabinet, or advisory body, is customarily made up of the heads of executive departments and other officers. **Senatorial courtesy** is a custom in which the Senate will not approve a presidential appointment to serve in a State if the appointment is opposed by a senator from the President's party.

Lesson Vocabulary

executive agreement   a pact made by the President directly with the head of a foreign state; a binding international agreement with the force of law but which (unlike a treaty) does not require Senate consent

treaty   a formal agreement between two or more sovereign states

electoral college   group of persons chosen in each State and the District of Columbia every four years who make a formal selection of the President and Vice President

senatorial courtesy   an unwritten rule that is closely followed in the Senate

TOPIC 3 LESSON 3

Lesson Summary
FEDERALISM–POWERS DIVIDED

Federalism is the system of government in which a written constitution divides the powers of government. The U.S. Constitution provides for the **division of powers** between two levels—the National Government and the States.

The National Government possesses **delegated powers**—powers specifically given by the Constitution. Most of these are **exclusive powers**, or powers that belong only to the National Government.

There are three kinds of delegated powers. **Expressed powers** are those listed in the Constitution. **Implied powers** are not listed but are suggested. **Inherent powers** are those that national governments have historically possessed, such as the regulation of immigration.

The Constitution also denies the National Government some powers. This is accomplished in three ways: 1) expressly, 2) as a result of silence, or 3) because those powers would threaten the existence of the federal system.

(Continues on the next page.)

Lesson Vocabulary

division of powers   basic principle of federalism; the constitutional provisions by which governmental powers are divided on a geographic basis (in the United States, between the National Government and the States)

delegated powers   those powers, expressed, implied, or inherent, granted to the National Government by the Constitution

exclusive powers   those powers that can be exercised by the National Government alone

expressed powers   those delegated powers of the National Government that are spelled out, expressly, in the Constitution; also called the "enumerated powers"

implied powers   those delegated powers of the National Government that are suggested by the expressed powers set out in the Constitution; those "necessary and proper" to carry out the expressed powers

inherent powers   powers the Constitution is presumed to have delegated to the National Government because it is the government of a sovereign state within the world community

MODIFIED CORNELL NOTES

The States' powers are called **reserved powers**. They are powers not already given to the National Government and not listed as powers the States may not have. For example, the States may decide how old people must be to get drivers' licenses. While the States have a huge amount of powers, just as the Constitution denies powers to the National Government, so it denies powers to the States.

Most of the powers that the Constitution delegates to the National Government are **exclusive powers** that can be exercised only by the National Government; they cannot be exercised by the States under any circumstances. Some powers delegated to the National Government are **concurrent powers**. The National Government shares these powers with the State governments.

Since some of the powers of the National and State governments overlap, the Supreme Court plays the key role of resolving disputes. As part of this job, it applies the Constitution's Supremacy Clause, which states that the Constitution is the "supreme Law of the Land."

Lesson Vocabulary

reserved powers   those powers that the Constitution does not grant to the National Government and does not deny to the States

exclusive powers   those powers which can be exercised by the National Government alone

concurrent powers   those powers that both the National Government and the States possess and exercise

Name _____ Class _____ Date _____

Lesson Summary
THE NATIONAL GOVERNMENT AND THE STATES

The Constitution says that the National Government must guarantee a "Republican Form of Government" and protect the States "against Invasion" and against "domestic Violence." This last statement allows federal officials to enter a State to restore order or to help in a disaster.

The National Government may create new States but not from the territory of an existing State without permission from that State's legislature. To become a new State, an area's residents must first ask Congress for admission. Congress passes an **enabling act**, which approves the writing of a State constitution. The area's residents write the constitution and submit it to Congress. Congress makes the area a State with an **act of admission**. When the President signs the act, the State is admitted to the Union.

The National Government and States cooperate in many ways. Through three types of **grants-in-aid** programs, the National Government gives resources to the States or their local governments. **Categorical grants** are made for specified purposes. **Block grants** are given for much broader purposes. **Project grants** are made to States, localities, and even private agencies that apply for them. In turn, States assist the National Government in many ways. For example, the State and local governments carry out and pay for national elections.

Trouble among the States was a major reason for the adoption of the Constitution. As a result, several parts of the document deal with how the States interact. For example, the Constitution forbids States to make treaties with one another. However, they may make **interstate compacts**, or agreements, in response to shared problems.

(Continues on the next page.)

Lesson Vocabulary

enabling act a congressional act directing the people of a United States territory to frame a proposed State constitution as a step toward admission to the Union

act of admission a congressional act admitting a new State to the Union

grants-in-aid grants of federal money or other resources to States, cities, counties, and other local units

categorical grants one type of federal grants-in-aid; made for some specific, closely defined purpose

block grants one type of federal grants-in-aid for some particular but broadly define area of public policy

project grants one type of federal grants-in-aid; made for specific projects to States, localities, and private agencies who apply for them

interstate compact formal agreement entered into with the consent of Congress, between or among States, or between a State and a foreign state

TOPIC 3 LESSON 4

Lesson Summary

THE NATIONAL GOVERNMENT AND THE STATES (continued)

The Full Faith and Credit Clause of the Constitution says that each State must honor the laws, records, and court decisions of every other State. This clause applies only to civil matters, not criminal matters.

The Constitution also establishes **extradition**, the legal process by which a person accused of a crime in one State is returned for trial to that State by the police of another State.

The Constitution's Privileges and Immunities Clause says that no State may discriminate against a person who lives in another State. Thus, each State must recognize the right of any American to travel in, do business in, or become a resident of that State. However, a State may draw reasonable distinctions between its own residents and those of other States. For example, a State may require that a person live within its boundaries for a period of time before voting.

The Constitution's provisions about interstate relations strengthened the hand of the National Government. By doing so, they lessened many of the frictions between the States.

Lesson Vocabulary

extradition   the legal process by which a fugitive from justice in one State is returned to that State

TOPIC 3 Review Questions
THE CONSTITUTION

Answer the questions below using the information in the Lesson Summaries on the previous pages.

Lesson 1: An Overview of the Constitution

1. Draw Inferences How do American citizens exercise popular sovereignty?

_____

_____

2. Assess an Opinion If there were no system of checks and balances, the process of government would eventually fall apart. Do you agree with this opinion? Why or why not?

_____

_____

Lesson 2: Amending the Constitution

3. Compare and Contrast What is similar about why Congress and the courts informally change the Constitution? How do their methods of changing the Constitution vary?

_____

_____

4. Identify Cause and Effect Thousands of amendments to the Constitution have been proposed. Why do you think only 27 formal amendments have been added to the Constitution?

_____

_____

Lesson 3: Federalism–Powers Divided

5. Does the Constitution specifically list powers that belong to the States? Explain your answer.

_____

_____

6. What are concurrent powers?

_____

_____

Lesson 4: The National Government and the States

7. Suppose a territory wants to become a new State. What is the first step that the residents of that territory must take?

_____

_____

8. Name one way that the National Government helps State and local governments and one way that State and local governments help the National Government.

_____

_____

TOPIC 4

Note Taking Study Guide

THE LEGISLATIVE BRANCH

Focus Question: How should government meet the needs of its people?

As you read, note ways in which members of Congress meet Americans' needs through legislation.

Meeting the People's Needs

I. What Members of Congress Do

  A.

  B. Represent the people of their state or district

  C. Protect creative Americans in science and the arts

    1.

    2.

  D. Help businesses

    1. by establishing a postal system

    2.

    3.

  E.

II. How Members of Congress Do It

  A. Select party leaders to manage legislation

  B.

  C.

  D.

  E. If needed, revise House and Senate versions of a bill through compromise

Lesson Summary
NATIONAL LEGISLATURE OVERVIEW

MODIFIED CORNELL NOTES

The Framers of the Constitution designed a National Government that put the legislature's power within a broader system of checks and balances. Congress is the legislative branch of the National Government that makes laws. Members of Congress carry out the following five key duties: they act as legislators, representatives of their constituents, committee members, servants of their constituents, and politicians. Typically, they take on one of four roles as they vote on bills. As **delegates**, they base their votes on the wishes of the "folks back home," their constituents. As **trustees**, they consider each bill's merits, regardless of the views of constituents. As **partisans**, they vote in line with their political party. As **politicos**, they consider all of these factors when they vote. Modern-day polling, the Internet, and the rise of "career legislators" have led many legislators to adhere to the delegate model today.

Members of Congress meet in committees to screen and decide which proposed laws, or **bills**, go on to **floor consideration**, the process whereby bills are considered and acted on by the full membership of each house. Members of Congress also exercise the **oversight function**, to verify that the executive branch is working effectively and in line with the policies that Congress has set. Members of Congress also act as servants of their constituents, helping those they represent solve problems regarding the National Government.

Most members of Congress are white, upper-middle class, and male, although more women and minorities have been elected in recent years. Most also have previous political experience, such as being a State governor or legislator.

(Continues on the next page.)

Lesson Vocabulary

delegates   members of Congress who cast votes based on the wishes of their constituents

trustees   lawmakers who vote based on their conscience and judgment, not the views of their constituents

partisans   lawmakers who owe their first allegiance to their political party and vote according to the party line

politicos   lawmakers who attempt to balance the basic elements of the trustee, delegate, and partisan roles

bills   proposed laws presented to a legislative body for consideration

floor consideration   the process by which proposed laws are considered and acted upon by the full membership of the House or Senate

oversight function   review by legislative committees of the policies and programs of the executive branch

Lesson Summary
NATIONAL LEGISLATURE OVERVIEW (continued)

MODIFIED CORNELL NOTES

The term of Congress is the length of time its officials serve after their election. Each term begins on January 3 of every odd-numbered year and lasts for two years. Congress holds one **session**, or meeting period, every year. Each term has two sessions. Congress can adjourn, or end, a session when it finishes its business. Today, Congress meets almost year-round, with several recesses, or breaks. The President has an as-yet-unused power to prorogue, or adjourn, a session if the two houses cannot agree on an adjournment date.

In case of an emergency, the President may call Congress into **special session**. Because Congress spends so much of the year in session, the President has not called a special session in over fifty years.

For their work, members of Congress receive a salary and benefits such as the franking privilege, the right to send mail postage free. Although the Constitution gives Congress the ability to fix its own salary, there are two limits on the level of congressional pay: the President's veto power and the fear of voter backlash. The latter is the more powerful limiting force.

Lesson Vocabulary

session period of time each year during which Congress assembles and conducts business

special session an extraordinary session of a legislative body, called to deal with an emergency situation

TOPIC 4
LESSON 2

Lesson Summary
THE TWO HOUSES

Today, the House of Representatives has 435 members. Congress **apportions**, or distributes, seats in the House among the States according to their populations. Each State sends at least one representative to the House.

Since the Reapportionment Act of 1929, seats in the House have been **reapportioned** or redistributed every 10 years when the United States counts its population. This population count is called a census. After each census has been conducted, the number of representatives of any State may change based on changes in its population. Once Congress decides how many House seats each State has, the State draws the boundaries of its electoral districts. Since 1842, the use of the **single-member district** arrangement has allowed the voters of each congressional district to choose one representative from a pool of candidates associated with that district. Before 1842, voters in some States chose their representatives **at-large**, or from the State as a whole. States must follow guidelines and avoid **gerrymandering**, or drawing districts in a way that is advantageous to the State legislature's controlling party.

Congressional elections are held in November of even-numbered years. An **off-year election** is a congressional election that is held between presidential elections. To become a representative, a person must be at least 25 years of age, a citizen of the United States for seven years, and a resident in the State that he or she wishes to represent. Representatives serve two-year terms and may be elected an unlimited number of times. Informal qualifications include party identification, name familiarity, gender, ethnic characteristics, and political experience. Being the incumbent, the person who currently holds the office, almost always helps win votes. Over 90 percent of those members of the House who seek reelection do so successfully.

(Continues on the next page.)

Lesson Vocabulary

apportion   distribute, as in seats in a legislative body

reapportion   redistribute, as in seats in a legislative body

single-member district   electoral district from which one person is chosen by the voters for each elected office

at-large   election of an officeholder by the voters of an entire governmental unit (e.g., a State or country) rather than by the voters of a district or subdivision

gerrymandering   the drawing of electoral district lines to the advantage of a party or group

off-year election   congressional election that occurs between presidential election years

TOPIC 4 LESSON 2

Lesson Summary
THE TWO HOUSES (continued)

The Senate has 100 members, two from each State—a number established by the Constitution. The Senate is therefore a much smaller body than the House of Representatives. The voters of each State elect one senator in any given election, unless the other seat has been vacated by death, resignation, or expulsion and so also needs to be filled.

The Senate is called the "upper house" of Congress because senators meet stricter qualifications and serve longer terms than representatives do. Senators serve six-year terms whose start dates are staggered so that only one-third of the senators' terms end at the same time. This means that every two years about 33 senators come up for reelection. The Senate is, therefore, a **continuous body**; it never contains only new members, so a majority of its membership always has experience. The longer terms for senators and the larger size and geographic diversity of their **constituencies**—those people who elect them—are designed to remove senators, at least somewhat, from day-to-day politics. In contrast to their colleagues, or coworkers, in the House, senators have more power and prestige and are more likely to be seen as national political leaders.

To become a senator, a person must be at least 30 years of age, a citizen of the United States for at least nine years, and a resident in the State that he or she wishes to represent. Senators must also meet the same informal qualifications as representatives.

Lesson Vocabulary

continuous body   governing unit (e.g., the United States Senate) whose seats are never all up for election at the same time

constituencies   the people and interests that an elected official represents

Lesson Summary
THE EXPRESSED POWERS

MODIFIED CORNELL NOTES

Article 1 of the Constitution describes Congress and grants it specific powers, which are called expressed powers. Those powers of Congress not listed in the Constitution but needed to carry out its **expressed powers** are **implied powers**. Congress also has **inherent powers** by its very nature as the National Government's legislative branch.

Congress's **commerce power** allows it to regulate both foreign and interstate trade. The Supreme Court has ruled that "trade" includes transportation and other ways in which people interact. However, Congress may not tax exports or favor one State over another.

The Constitution gives Congress several powers related to money. Congress has the power to **tax**—to impose a charge on people or property in order to fund public needs. Tax collecting must, however, be used in accord with all other provisions of the Constitution. Over ninety percent of the revenue of the National Government comes from taxes, of which there are two kinds—direct taxes and indirect taxes. Direct taxes are paid directly by the taxed person. Income tax is a direct tax. Indirect taxes are first paid by one person, such as a manufacturer, and are then passed on to others, such as consumers. The Constitution allows Congress to borrow money. While there is a legal ceiling on the public debt, or money borrowed and still owed by the nation, the National Government has long spent more than it takes in and borrows each year. This practice, called **deficit financing**, has led to a very large public debt.

(Continues on the next page.)

Lesson Vocabulary

expressed powers   those delegated powers of the National Government that are spelled out, expressly, in the Constitution; also called the "enumerated powers"

implied powers   those delegated powers of the National Government that are suggested by the expressed powers set out in the Constitution; those "necessary and proper" to carry out the expressed powers

inherent powers   those powers the Constitution is presumed to have delegated to the National Government because it is the government of a sovereign state within the world community

commerce power   exclusive power of Congress to regulate interstate and foreign trade

tax   a charge levied by government on persons or property to raise money to meet public needs

deficit financing   the practice of funding government by borrowing to make up the difference between government spending and revenue

TOPIC 4 LESSON 3

Lesson Summary
THE EXPRESSED POWERS (continued)

Congress may also make laws about **bankruptcy**. A bankrupt person, company, or organization is one a court finds insolvent, or unable to pay bills. Bankruptcy is the legal process by which the assets are divided among those owed. Finally, Congress has the power to coin money. Money made by the government is called legal tender, or money that by law must be accepted in payment of debts.

The Constitution grants Congress other domestic powers as well. Congress promotes science and the arts by protecting the work of both writers and inventors through copyright laws. A **copyright** is the exclusive right of an author to reproduce, publish, and sell his or her work. A **patent** gives an inventor the sole right to make, use, or sell "any new and useful art, machine, manufacture…or any new and useful improvement thereof." Congress has the power to establish a system to carry the mail and has used this power to pass laws against crimes involving the postal system. Congress can acquire, manage, and dispose of various federal areas, including the District of Columbia and federal territories, parts of the United States that are not admitted as States and that have their own systems of government, including Puerto Rico, Guam, and the Virgin Islands. The Federal Government may take private property for public use by **eminent domain**. Congress has the power to fix standards for weights and measures for the country and to make laws about naturalization, or the process by which foreigners become U.S. citizens. Finally, Congress has the power to establish all federal courts below the Supreme Court and to define federal crimes and set the punishments that may be imposed on those who violate federal law.

The Federal Government has greater powers in the field of foreign policy than it does in any other area. This power arises from its spending, commerce, and war powers. The President can commit American military forces to combat abroad, but only Congress can declare war. It alone has the power to raise and support armies, to provide and maintain a navy, and to make rules for the governing of the nation's military forces.

Lesson Vocabulary

bankruptcy   the legal proceeding by which a bankrupt person's assets are distributed among those to whom he or she owes debts

copyright   the exclusive, legal right of a person to reproduce, publish, and sell his or her own literary, musical, or artistic creations

patent   a license issued to an inventor granting the exclusive right to manufacture, use, or sell his or her invention for a limited period of time

eminent domain   the power of a government to take private property for public use

TOPIC **4** LESSON 4	**Lesson Summary**
	THE IMPLIED AND NONLEGISLATIVE POWERS

MODIFIED CORNELL NOTES

Congress's implied powers come from the Constitution's Necessary and Proper Clause. This clause grants Congress all the powers "necessary and proper" for executing its expressed powers. The clause is also called the Elastic Clause because its use has greatly stretched Congress's powers.

The battle over implied powers began in the 1790s. Strict constructionists, led by Thomas Jefferson, thought that the government should use only those powers *absolutely* necessary to carry out the expressed powers. **Liberal constructionists**, led by Alexander Hamilton, wanted a broad, or liberal, interpretation of the powers of Congress and believed that a good government is an active one. The liberal constructionists won. Over the years, Congress has acquired more powers than the Framers could ever have imagined. Wars, economic crises, and improvements in communication and transportation contributed to the growth of national power. Americans have generally agreed with, or come to **consensus** about, the scope of powers assumed by Congress.

Congress has found a basis for the exercise of implied powers in the commerce power, the power to tax and spend, and the war powers. The Commerce Clause gives Congress the right to regulate foreign and interstate trade. The word "commerce" has been held to include the production, sale, and purchase of goods as well as the transportation of people and commodities. This definition includes virtually all economic activity. Still, there are limits on what Congress can do under the Commerce Clause. Congress cannot pass a law based solely on the grounds that a measure will somehow promote "the general welfare of the United States." But it can and does levy taxes and provide for the spending of money for that purpose. For example, although the Constitution says nothing about education, Congress **appropriates**, or assigns to a particular use, billions of dollars for education every year. And, as with its other expressed powers, Congress has the authority to do whatever is necessary and proper for the execution of its war power, as long as it does not violate another provision of the Constitution.

(Continues on the next page.)

Lesson Vocabulary

liberal constructionist   one who argues for a broad interpretation of the Constitution's provisions, particularly those granting powers to the Federal Government

consensus   general agreement among various groups on fundamental matters; broad agreement on public questions

appropriates   assigns to a particular use

TOPIC 4 — LESSON 4

Lesson Summary
THE IMPLIED AND NONLEGISLATIVE POWERS (continued)

Congress also has the power to investigate, or to look into, any matter that falls within the scope of its lawmaking authority. The Senate has the power to approve all major presidential appointments and treaties entered into by the President. The House has the sole power to impeach, or accuse and bring formal charges, but the Senate has the sole power to try, or judge, impeachment cases. Two Presidents—Andrew Johnson and Bill Clinton—have been impeached. The Senate voted to acquit, that is, it found both men not guilty. Clinton's inappropriate relationship with a White House intern led to two articles of impeachment being brought against him. The first charged the President with **perjury**, or lying under oath. While many House members argued that Clinton's actions did not justify removal from office, some opponents pushed for a resolution to censure, or offer a formal condemnation, of his behavior.

Richard Nixon resigned from office in the face of certain impeachment as a result of the Watergate scandal. After a lengthy probe into a break-in attempt at the Democratic Party's national headquarters revealed a long list of illegal actions, the House Judiciary Committee voted three articles of impeachment against President Nixon in late July 1974. He was charged with obstruction of justice, abuse of power, and failure to respond to the Judiciary Committee's subpoenas. A committee's **subpoena** is a legal order directing one to appear before that body and/or to produce certain evidence. It was apparent that the House would impeach President Nixon and that the Senate would convict him. Those facts prompted Mr. Nixon to resign the presidency on August 9, 1974.

Finally, Congress may propose amendments by a two-thirds vote in each house. Also, if no presidential or vice-presidential candidate receives a majority of the electoral votes, the House may elect a President and the Senate may elect the Vice President. If a vacancy occurs in the vice presidency, the President may name a **successor**, or replacement, but the approval of both houses is required for approval.

Lesson Vocabulary

perjury   the act of lying under oath

subpoena   an order for a person to appear and to produce documents or other requested materials

successor   a person who inherits a title or office

TOPIC 4
LESSON 5

Lesson Summary
CONGRESS AT WORK—ORGANIZATION AND COMMITTEES

When Congress starts a new term, the House reorganizes because new members are taking seats. The members elect their leader, who swears in all the members. They adopt their work rules and appoint the members of their permanent committees. The Senate does not need to reorganize because two-thirds of its members stay the same from term to term. Within a few weeks, the President delivers the annual State of the Union message to a joint session of Congress. In this constitutionally mandated speech, the President reports on the state of the nation and lays out the policies and course the administration expects to follow.

Presiding over the House is the **Speaker of the House**, who is the majority party's leader and the most powerful person in Congress. The Speaker refers bills to committee, names the members of all select and conference committees, and may debate or vote on any matter before the House. The Speaker follows the Vice President in the line of presidential succession.

The Vice President of the United States acts as **president of the Senate**. The Vice President oversees the Senate's sessions but cannot debate and votes only in a tie. Unlike the Speaker of the House, the Vice President is not elected to the role. He or she is not a member of the Senate and may not be a member of the party that controls the Senate. In the Vice President's absence, the **president** *pro tempore* presides.

(Continues on the next page.)

Lesson Vocabulary

Speaker of the House   the presiding officer of the House of Representatives, chosen by and from the majority party in the House

president of the Senate   the presiding officer of a senate; in Congress, the Vice President of the United States; in a State's legislature, either the lieutenant governor or a Senator

president *pro tempore*   the presiding officer of a senate; in Congress, the Vice President of the United States; in a State's legislature, either the lieutenant governor or a Senator

TOPIC 4 LESSON 5

Lesson Summary

CONGRESS AT WORK—ORGANIZATION AND COMMITTEES
(continued)

Next to the Speaker, Congress's most powerful leaders are the majority and minority party **floor leaders**, the parties' chief spokespeople. They are selected during the **party caucuses**—meetings of the members of each party just before Congress convenes. The floor leaders help pass laws that their parties want. The floor leader of the party that holds the majority of seats in each house of Congress is known as the **majority leader**. The floor leader of the party that holds the minority of seats in each house is the **minority leader**. The two floor leaders are aided by party **whips**, or assistant floor leaders.

Committee chairmen are also powerful in Congress. They head the standing committees that do most of Congress's work. Each is almost always that committee's longest-standing member from the majority party. This custom is part of the **seniority rule**, which gives the most important posts in Congress to party members who have served the longest.

Lesson Vocabulary

floor leaders   members of the House and Senate picked by their parties to carry out party decisions and steer legislative action to meet party goals

party caucuses   a closed meeting of a party's house or senate members; also called a party conference

majority leader   the floor leader of the party that holds the majority of seats in each house of Congress

minority leader   the floor leader of the party that holds the minority of seats in each house of Congress

whips   assistants to the floor leaders in the House and Senate, responsible for monitoring and marshaling votes

committee chairman   member who heads a standing committee in a legislative body

seniority rule   unwritten rule in both houses of Congress reserving the top posts in each chamber, particularly committee chairmanships, for members with the longest records of service

Lesson Summary
CONGRESS AT WORK–MAKING LAW

Congress considers thousands of bills and resolutions at each session. A **bill** is a proposed law that applies to the nation as a whole or to certain people or places. **Joint resolutions** are similar to bills; when joint resolutions are passed, they have the force of law. They usually deal with unusual or temporary matters and have been used to propose amendments or annex territories. **Concurrent resolutions** lack the force of law and deal with matters in which the House and Senate must act jointly. **Resolutions**, often called "simple resolutions," deal with matters concerning one house alone and are taken up only by that body. They are used for such matters as the adoption of a new rule of procedure or the amendment of some existing rule. Like concurrent resolutions, a resolution does not have the force of law and is not sent to the President for approval. A bill or resolution usually deals with only one topic, but a **rider** regarding an unrelated matter may be included. A rider is a proposal with little chance of passing on its own, so it is attached to a bill that probably will pass. Riders are often tacked onto appropriations measures and called "earmarks."

After a bill is introduced, it is read. The Speaker then sends the bill to the appropriate standing committee. The committee may then act on the bill or set it aside and ignore it. Most of the thousands of bills introduced in each session of Congress are **pigeonholed**. That is, they are buried; they die in committee. A **discharge petition**, approved by a House majority, may force such a bill to the floor for debate.

(Continues on the next page.)

Lesson Vocabulary

bill   a proposed law presented to a legislative body for consideration

joint resolution   a proposal for action that has the force of law when passed; usually deals with special circumstances or temporary matters

concurrent resolution   a statement of position on an issue used by the House and Senate acting jointly; does not have the force of law and does not require the President's signature

resolution   a measure relating to the business of either house of Congress or expressing an opinion; does not have the force of law and does not require the President's signature

rider   unpopular provision added to an important bill certain to pass so it will "ride" through the legislative process

pigeonholed   expression describing how most bills introduced in each session of Congress are buried, put away, or never acted upon

discharge petition   enables members to force a bill that has remained in committee 30 days (7 for the Rules Committee) onto the floor for consideration

MODIFIED CORNELL NOTES

TOPIC 4 · LESSON 6

Lesson Summary
CONGRESS AT WORK—MAKING LAW (continued)

Once out of committee, a bill is placed on a calendar, or schedule for debating bills. Before the bill is debated, the House Rules Committee must approve it or it dies.

Once on the floor, the bill is read again. To speed the process, the entire House may debate it as a Committee of the Whole—one large committee that has less strict rules than does the House. This process is faster because the quorum, the number of members required to do business, is smaller for a Committee of the Whole than for the House.

Finally, a vote takes place. If approved, the bill is engrossed, or printed in final form. It is read once more and if approved is sent to the Senate.

In the Senate, a bill follows the same steps that it does in the House. However, most Senate procedures are less formal than those of the House.

Unlike the House, the Senate allows debate on bills to go on until all senators agree to end it. If one senator does not agree, debate continues and may result in a filibuster, a process in which a senator delays Senate action by talking at great length. The Senate can stop a filibuster only if three-fifths of the senators vote for cloture, or limiting debate.

For Congress to send a bill to the President, both houses must have passed identical versions of it. If necessary, a conference committee works out a compromise version that both houses will approve.

The President has ten days to act on a bill. He may sign the bill, and it becomes a law. He may veto—refuse to sign—the bill and send it back to Congress. The bill then dies unless both houses approve it again by a two-thirds vote. The President may also allow the bill to become law without a signature by not acting on it within the ten-day period. Lastly, if Congress adjourns its session within ten days of submitting a bill to the President, and the President has not signed the bill, the bill dies, a possibility called the **pocket veto**.

Lesson Vocabulary

pocket veto   a type of veto a chief executive may use after a legislature has adjourned when the chief executive does not sign or reject a bill within the time allowed to do so

TOPIC 4 — Review Questions
THE LEGISLATIVE BRANCH

Answer the questions below using the information in the Lesson Summaries on the previous pages.

Lesson 1: National Legislature Overview

1. Compare and Contrast If you were a member of Congress, would you tend to vote as a "delegate" or as a "trustee"? Explain your answer.

_____

_____

2. Draw Inferences Why is Congress's oversight function considered to be an important part of the American system of checks and balances?

_____

_____

Lesson 2: The Two Houses

3. Draw Inferences Would you expect the borders of a gerrymandered district to appear on a map as a rectangle or circle or some other recognizable shape? Why or why not?

_____

_____

4. Compare and Contrast What are the formal qualifications for someone who wishes to serve in the House of Representatives? How do those compare with the qualifications for serving in the Senate?

_____

_____

Lesson 3: The Expressed Powers

5. Draw Inferences The Constitution gives Congress the commerce power, but it specifically states that Congress may not tax exports. Why do you think the Constitution placed that limit on Congress?

_____

_____

6. Who would most likely apply for a copyright? Who would most likely apply for a patent?

_____

_____

Lesson 4: The Implied and Nonlegislative Powers

7. Draw Conclusions What is the Necessary and Proper Clause? Explain how this clause gives Congress flexibility in making laws.

_____

_____

8. What is the name of the clause in the Constitution that gives Congress the right to regulate foreign and interstate trade?

_____

_____

Lesson 5: Congress at Work–Organization and Committees

9. What do floor leaders in Congress do?

_____

_____

10. Assess an Argument Do you agree with the seniority rule? Why or why not?

_____

_____

Lesson 6: Congress at Work–Making Law

11. Why might a member of Congress attach a rider to a bill?

_____

_____

12. Draw Conclusions What role does a conference committee play in the process of making law? Why is it important that such a committee exists in the legislative branch?

_____

_____

_____

TOPIC 5

Note Taking Study Guide

THE EXECUTIVE BRANCH—THE PRESIDENCY AND VICE PRESIDENCY

Focus Question: What makes a good leader?

As you read, note the abilities that a good President must have.

Presidential Leadership			
Ability to play many executive roles	**Ability to choose reliable supporters**	**Ability to execute domestic powers**	**Ability to execute foreign affairs powers**
•	•	•	•
•	• First Lady	•	•
•	•	• veto power	•
• chief diplomat			•
•			
•			
•			
•			

TOPIC 5 LESSON 1

Lesson Summary
THE PRESIDENCY: AN OVERVIEW

The Constitution grants the President six of his nine roles. The President acts as the ceremonial head of the government, or **chief of state**. As such, he stands as the representative of all the people of the nation. The President is also head of the executive branch, or **chief executive**. As **chief administrator**, he manages the Federal Government. As the nation's **chief diplomat**, the President sets the nation's foreign policy. The President directly controls all U.S. military forces as the **commander in chief**. He determines Congress's agenda in his role as **chief legislator**.

Three presidential roles are not defined by the Constitution. As **chief economist**, the President monitors the nation's domestic and international economy and takes action as necessary. The President is also **chief of party**, the unofficial head of his political party. Finally, the President is also **chief citizen**, and, as such, is expected to work for and to represent the public interest.

To become President, a person must be a natural-born citizen, at least 35 years old, and a resident of the United States for at least 14 years. In 1951, the 22nd Amendment limited the presidency to two terms of four years each.

(Continues on the next page.)

Lesson Vocabulary

chief of state   term for the President as the ceremonial head of the United States, the symbol of all the people of the nation

chief executive   term for the President as vested with the executive power of the United States

chief administrator   term for the President as head of the administration of the Federal Government

chief diplomat   term for the President as the main architect of foreign policy and spokesperson to other countries

commander in chief   term for the President as commander of the nation's armed forces

chief legislator   term for the President as architect of public policy and the one who sets the agenda for Congress

chief economist   term for the President as monitor of the nation's economic condition

chief of party   term for the President as the leader of his or her political party

chief citizen   term for the President as the representative of the people, working for the public interest

TOPIC 5 LESSON 1 — Lesson Summary
THE PRESIDENCY: AN OVERVIEW (continued)

The plan by which a presidential vacancy is filled is known as **presidential succession**. The 25th Amendment says that the Vice President will become President if the President dies, resigns, or is removed from office. If the Vice President is unable to serve, the Presidential Succession Act of 1947 says the Speaker of the House and the Senate's president *pro tempore* are the next officers in line.

The 25th Amendment also states that the Vice President becomes acting President if the President tells Congress he or she cannot do his or her job, or if the Vice President and a majority of the Cabinet tell Congress that the President is disabled. The President may return to the job at a later point when ready. If the Vice President and a majority of the Cabinet disagree, Congress must decide if the disability still exists.

Lesson Vocabulary

presidential succession   scheme by which a presidential vacancy is filled

Name _____ Class _____ Date _____

MODIFIED CORNELL NOTES

The Constitution pays little attention to the office of the Vice President. It assigns the Vice President two roles: he or she presides over the Senate and helps to decide the question of presidential disability. Political parties usually pick a candidate for Vice President who will **balance the ticket**, or help the presidential candidate appeal to a broader range of voters. In recent years, Vice Presidents have been given more responsibility. The 25th Amendment states that if the office of Vice President becomes vacant, the President chooses a replacement who must then be confirmed by a majority vote in both houses.

   First Lady is the official title of the President's wife. The First Lady provides informal advice, advocates for particular policies, and performs a number of symbolic functions.

Lesson Vocabulary

balance the ticket   when a presidential candidate chooses a running mate who can strengthen his chance of being elected by virtue of certain ideological, geographical, racial, ethnic, gender, or other characteristics

First Lady   the President's wife

TOPIC 5 LESSON 3 — Lesson Summary
THE PRESIDENT'S DOMESTIC POWERS

The Constitution's Executive Article, Article II, gives the President some specific powers, but it gives few details about them. Debate about the extent of these powers began with the Framers and has continued since.

Over time, the presidency has become very powerful for several reasons. First, the presidency has changed as a result of the Presidents themselves. Second, as the executive office has expanded in size and scope, so have the powers of the President. Third, as American life has grown more complex, citizens have looked to the President for leadership on such issues as the economy and healthcare. Fourth, in national emergencies, the President, as commander in chief, has needed to take decisive action. Fifth, Congress has passed many laws that expand the Federal Government's activities. Not having time itself, Congress has had to ask the executive branch to carry out these laws.

Despite the expanded scope of the presidency, no President can become all-powerful. The Constitution and Congress both provide powerful checks on executive power. Some past Presidents have taken a broad view of their powers, while others have said the President should have limited power. Critics of strong presidential power have used the term the "imperial presidency" to compare the President to an emperor who takes strong actions without Congress's—or the people's—approval.

The President is the head of the executive branch and must carry out the provisions of federal law. The power to do so comes partly from the Constitution and partly from the oath of office—the solemn promise that each President takes at the inauguration to "preserve, protect, and defend the Constitution." The President's executive power offers him or her many chances to decide how laws are carried out.

The President possesses **ordinance power**, the power to issue executive orders. An **executive order** is a directive, rule, or regulation that has the effect of law. The Constitution does not expressly give the President this power, but the President must be able to issue orders to implement his or her constitutional powers. Congress backs up this implied power by regularly authorizing the President to use it.

(Continues on the next page.)

Lesson Vocabulary

ordinance power   power of the President to issue executive orders; originates from the Constitution and acts of Congress

executive order   directive, rule, or regulation issued by a chief executive or subordinates, based upon constitutional or statutory authority and having the force of law

TOPIC 5
LESSON 3

Lesson Summary
THE PRESIDENT'S DOMESTIC POWERS (continued)

MODIFIED CORNELL NOTES

In order to have loyal subordinates, the President can choose the top officials of the executive branch, including heads of executive agencies, diplomats, Cabinet members, federal judges, and military officers. The Senate must approve these appointments with a majority vote. For State officials, the custom of senatorial courtesy holds that the Senate will approve only those appointments accepted by the State's senator from the President's party.

The President alone has the power to fire executive officials. However, the President may not remove federal judges and generally can only remove people whom he or she has appointed.

Various Presidents have insisted that the Constitution gives the President the power to refuse to disclose certain information to Congress or to the federal courts. That is, they have claimed the power of executive privilege. Congress has never recognized executive privilege, but the Supreme Court has recognized it.

The Constitution also grants the President certain judicial powers. It authorizes the President to grant "reprieves and pardons for offenses against the United States, except in cases of impeachment." A **reprieve** is the postponement of the execution of a sentence. A **pardon** is legal forgiveness for a crime. The pardoning power includes the powers of commutation and amnesty. **Commutation** is the power to reduce the length of a sentence or the amount of a fine imposed by a court. **Amnesty** is a general pardon offered to a group of law violators. These powers of **clemency**, that is, leniency or mercy, may only be used in cases involving federal offenses.

(Continues on the next page.)

Lesson Vocabulary

reprieve   an official postponement of the execution of a sentence

pardon   release from the punishment or legal consequences of a crime by the President (in a federal case) or a governor (in a State case)

commutation   the power to reduce (commute) the length of a sentence or fine for a crime

amnesty   a blanket pardon offered to a group of law violators

clemency   mercy or leniency granted to an offender by a chief executive

Lesson Summary

THE PRESIDENT'S DOMESTIC POWERS (continued)

Because of the President's legislative powers, he or she may tell Congress what laws the nation needs. The President proposes some laws in an annual State of the Union address and others in an annual budget plan and economic report.

Once Congress passes a bill, the President has ten days to act on it. The President can sign the bill to make it law, allow it to become law without a signature, **veto** it and thereby send it back to Congress, or use the pocket veto to let it die by not signing it before Congress adjourns. Also, from 1996 to 1998 the President had the power to use a **line-item veto** on spending and tax bills. This allowed the President to approve most of a bill while vetoing certain parts, called line items.

Lesson Vocabulary

veto chief executive's power to reject a bill passed by a legislature; literally (Latin) "I forbid"

line-item veto a President's cancellation of specific dollar amounts (line items) from a congressional spending bill; instituted by a 1996 congressional act, but struck down by a 1998 Supreme Court decision

TOPIC
5
LESSON 4

Lesson Summary
THE PRESIDENT'S FOREIGN AFFAIRS POWERS

The President is in charge of foreign affairs for the United States. He can make a **treaty**, or formal agreement, with another nation, which must be approved by a two-thirds vote of the Senate. However, the President may avoid needing senatorial approval by making an **executive agreement**, or pact, with another nation's leader.

The President also has the power of **recognition**, which is to acknowledge—and by implication support—the legal existence of another country and its government. Nations generally recognize each other by exchanging diplomatic representatives. One nation may show its strong disapproval of another by calling back its ambassador and sending the other's ambassador home. The official recalled is said to be **persona non grata**, or an unwelcome person.

The power to declare war belongs to Congress. However, as commander in chief, the President can still make war. More than 200 times, a President has sent U.S. forces into combat without a congressional declaration of war. After the undeclared Vietnam War, Congress passed the War Powers Resolution of 1973, designed to limit the President's war-making powers. It states that combat must cease after sixty days without the authorization of Congress.

Lesson Vocabulary

treaty   a formal agreement between two or more sovereign states

executive agreement   a pact made by the President directly with the head of a foreign state; a binding international agreement with the force of law but which (unlike a treaty) does not require Senate consent

recognition   the exclusive power of a President to legally recognize (establish formal diplomatic relations with) foreign states

persona non grata   an unwelcome person; used to describe recalled diplomatic officials

TOPIC 5 — Review Questions
THE EXECUTIVE BRANCH—THE PRESIDENCY AND VICE PRESIDENCY

Answer the questions below using the information in the Lesson Summaries on the previous pages.

Lesson 1: The Presidency: An Overview

1. Which of the President's nine roles calls for him to set the nation's foreign policy?

_____

_____

2. Draw Conclusions What are the formal qualifications for the office of President, and why do you think the Framers specified these requirements?

_____

_____

Lesson 2: The Vice President and the First Lady

3. What are the Vice President's two main roles?

_____

_____

4. Draw Inferences Why do you think the President's wife is called the First Lady?

_____

_____

Lesson 3: The President's Domestic Powers

5. What prevents a President from becoming an all-powerful dictator?

_____

_____

6. Identify Causes and Effects The Constitution does not specify the President's ordinance power. What might happen if Presidents could not use this power?

_____

_____

Lesson 4: The President's Foreign Affairs Powers

7. Identify Supporting Details The system of checks and balances helps keep any one branch from gaining too much power. How is that system applied to the President's treaty-making power?

_____

_____

8. Why did Congress pass the War Powers Resolution of 1973?

_____

_____

TOPIC 6

Note Taking Study Guide

THE EXECUTIVE BRANCH AT WORK

Focus Question: What should governments do?

As you read, note how the structure of the executive branch illustrates the many things that government is responsible for.

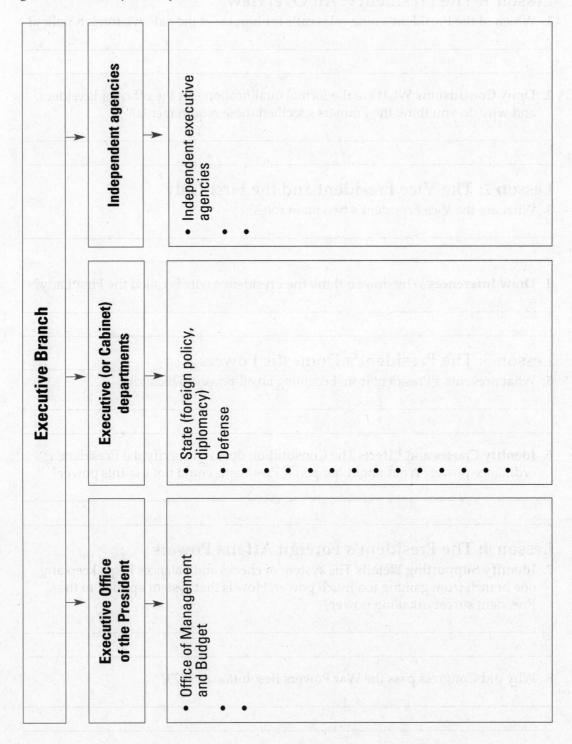

Executive Branch

Independent agencies
- Independent executive agencies
  - •
  - •
  - •

Executive (or Cabinet) departments
- State (foreign policy, diplomacy)
- Defense
  - • • • • • • • • • • • • • • • • •

Executive Office of the President
- Office of Management and Budget
  - •
  - •
  - •

TOPIC 6 · LESSON 1

Lesson Summary

THE FEDERAL BUREAUCRACY

A **bureaucracy** is a large, complex structure that handles the everyday business of an organization. It is founded on three principles. First, a bureaucracy has a hierarchical structure—a few top officials and units have authority over a large group of managers, who, in turn, supervise many more workers. Second, each **bureaucrat**, or person who works for the organization, has a specific job. Third, a bureaucracy operates under a set of formalized rules.

The federal bureaucracy is all the agencies, people, and procedures through which the Federal Government operates. The President is its chief administrator. His **administration** consists of the government's many agencies and administrators. The executive branch is composed of three groups of agencies: the Executive Office of the President, the fifteen Cabinet departments, and many independent agencies.

The units of the bureaucracy go by multiple names. The term *department* is used for agencies of Cabinet rank. *Agencies* and *administrations* have near-Cabinet status and are each overseen by an administrator. *Commissions* regulate business activities and may advise on or investigate other concerns. Authorities and corporations conduct business-like activities under a board and a manager.

Each administrative organization is made up of one of two types of units. **Staff agencies** provide support for other workers and assist in the management of an organization. **Line agencies** perform an organization's tasks.

Lesson Vocabulary

bureaucracy   a large, complex administrative structure that handles the everyday business of an organization

bureaucrat   a person who works for a bureaucratic organization

administration   the officials in the executive branch of a government and their policies and principles

staff agency   agency that supports the chief executive and other administrators by offering advice and other assistance in the management of an organization

line agency   agency that perform the tasks for which an organization exists

TOPIC 6 LESSON 2

Lesson Summary

THE EOP AND THE EXECUTIVE DEPARTMENTS

The Executive Office of the President (EOP) is a complex organization of agencies staffed by most of the President's closest advisors and assistants.

The White House Office is the "nerve center" of the EOP. It includes the President's chief of staff, who directs White House operations, and other key members of the President's inner circle.

As part of the EOP, the National Security Council advises the President in all matters that relate to the nation's safety. The President chairs the council.

The EOP's largest unit is the Office of Management and Budget (OMB), which prepares the **federal budget**. This budget gives a detailed estimate of the money to be received and spent by the Federal Government during the coming **fiscal year**. A fiscal year is the twelve-month period used by a government or business for financial management. The Federal Government's fiscal year begins on October 1.

The EOP also includes other agencies such as the Office of National Drug Control Policy, which oversees federal efforts to fight drugs. Three of the nation's leading economists make up the Council of Economic Advisers. Still other units of the EOP deal directly with **domestic affairs**, or matters confined within the States.

Much of the Federal Government's work is carried out by the fifteen **executive departments**, the traditional units of federal administration that are often called the Cabinet departments. The Cabinet is an informal advisory board convened by the President to serve his or her needs; it is made up of the heads of each executive department and other top officials. The Cabinet departments employ nearly two-thirds of the federal **civilian**, or nonmilitary, workforce.

(Continues on the next page.)

Lesson Vocabulary

federal budget   a detailed financial document containing estimates of federal income and spending during the coming fiscal year

fiscal year   the 12-month period used by a government and the business world for its record-keeping, budgeting, revenue-collecting, and other financial management purposes

domestic affairs   all matters not directly connected to the realm of foreign affairs

executive departments   often called the Cabinet departments, they are the traditional units of federal administration

civilian   nonmilitary

TOPIC 6 LESSON 2

Lesson Summary

THE EOP AND THE EXECUTIVE DEPARTMENTS (continued)

Each department head is called a secretary, except for the head of the Department of Justice, who is the attorney general. These heads act as the primary links between the President and the subunits within their departments. The President chooses each department head, but these appointments must be confirmed by the Senate.

Today, the executive departments vary in terms of visibility, importance, and size. The Department of State is the oldest and most prestigious department, but it is also the smallest. The Department of Defense is the largest. The Department of Health and Human Services has the largest budget, and the Department of Homeland Security is the newest. The other departments are those of the Treasury, Justice, the Interior, Agriculture, Commerce, Labor, Housing and Urban Development, Transportation, Energy, Education, and Veterans Affairs.

Cabinet members are appointed by the President and subject to confirmation by the Senate. While professional qualifications and practical experience influence choices, so do gender, race, ethnicity, and geography. Once a central cog in presidential government, the importance of the Cabinet has declined in recent years.

MODIFIED CORNELL NOTES

TOPIC 6
LESSON 3

Lesson Summary
THE INDEPENDENT AGENCIES

Since the 1880s, Congress has created many **independent agencies**, or agencies that operate outside the executive Cabinet departments. These agencies exist for a number of reasons. Some agencies do not fit well in any department. Some need protection from department politics. Others must be independent because of the nature of their functions.

Three main types of independent agencies exist today. Most are **independent executive agencies**. Independent executive agencies are organized like executive departments with subunits and a single head, but they do not have Cabinet status. NASA (National Space and Aeronautics Administration) is an independent executive agency. Created to oversee the nation's space programs, its scientific research has led to numerous advances in the civilian realm. The OPM (Office of Personnel Management) is the nation's largest employer, hiring, employing, and promoting thousands of civilian career workers in the civil service. The **civil service**, which bases hiring and promotion on merit, was meant to end the **patronage system**, which gave jobs to political supporters and friends and resulted in inefficiency and corruption. The Selective Service System, a third type of independent executive agency, manages the **draft**, or required military service. The first national draft occurred in 1917, when the Selective Service Act drafted men to fight in World War I. Between 1940 and 1973, the draft was the major source of military personnel in the United States. Although the draft ended in 1973, young men must still register for the draft soon after their 18th birthday.

(Continues on the next page.)

Lesson Vocabulary

independent agencies   additional agencies created by Congress located outside the Cabinet departments

independent executive agencies   agencies headed by a single administrator with regional subunits but lacking Cabinet status

civil service   those civilian employees who perform the administrative work of government

patronage system   the practice of giving jobs to supporters and friends

draft   conscription, or compulsory military service

TOPIC 6 LESSON 3 — Lesson Summary
THE INDEPENDENT AGENCIES (continued)

Independent agencies that regulate aspects of the economy are called **independent regulatory commissions**. They are unique because they exist outside of presidential control and are quasi-legislative and quasi-judicial. This means that Congress has given them certain legislative-like and judicial-like powers. Legislatively, they may make rules detailing laws that Congress has asked them to enforce; these rules carry the force of law. Judicially, they may decide disputes in the fields in which Congress has given them policing authority.

Some independent agencies are known as **government corporations**. These agencies, such as the U.S. Postal Service, carry out certain business-like activities.

Lesson Vocabulary

independent regulatory commissions   independent agencies created by Congress, designed to regulate important aspects of the nation's economy, largely beyond the reach of presidential control

government corporations   corporations within the executive branch subject to the President's direction and control, set up by Congress to carry out certain business-like activities

Name _____ Class _____ Date _____

MODIFIED CORNELL NOTES

A nation's **foreign policy** is every aspect of its relationships with other countries—military, diplomatic, commercial, and all others. The President takes the lead in making and carrying out U.S. foreign policy.

For over 150 years, Americans were more interested in **domestic affairs**—events happening in the United States—than in **foreign affairs**—events involving other countries. During that time, the United States practiced a policy of **isolationism**, or a refusal to become engaged in foreign affairs. In 1823, the Monroe Doctrine stated that the United States would keep itself out of European affairs and that European nations should stay out of the affairs of North and South America. The United States was active in the Western Hemisphere, however. In the 1800s, it began expanding its territory. By winning the Spanish-American War in 1898, the United States gained colonial territories and began to emerge as a world power. Under what came to be known as the Roosevelt Corollary to the Monroe Doctrine, the United States began to police Latin America in the early 1900s. This policy took a dramatic turn in the 1930s with Franklin Roosevelt's Good Neighbor Policy, a conscious attempt to win friends to the south by reducing this nation's political and military interventions in the region.

(Continues on the next page.)

Lesson Vocabulary

foreign policy   a group of policies made up of all the stands and actions that a nation takes in every aspect of its relationships with other countries; everything a nation's government says and does in world affairs

domestic affairs   all matters not directly connected to the realm of foreign affairs

foreign affairs   a nation's relationships with other countries

isolationism   a purposeful refusal to become generally involved in the affairs of the rest of the world

TOPIC 6 LESSON 4

Lesson Summary

FOREIGN POLICY OVERVIEW (continued)

In the early 1900s, the United States began forming more international relationships, such as that with China. World War II brought a final end to U.S. isolationism. Most nations at that point turned to the principle of **collective security**, by which they agreed to act together against any nation that threatened the peace. The United States also took up a policy of **deterrence**—building military strength to discourage attack. This policy began during the **cold war**—more than forty years of hostile relations between the United States and the Soviet Union.

During the cold war, the United States supported a policy of **containment**, the notion that if communism could be contained within its existing boundaries, it would collapse under the weight of its internal weaknesses. As the United States withdrew from the Vietnam War, it began a policy of **détente**—"a relaxation of tensions"—that improved relations with the Soviet Union and China.

The end of the cold war began when Mikhail Gorbachev became the leader of the Soviet Union. United States-Soviet relations had improved significantly by the time the Soviet Union collapsed in 1991. Since then, some key events shaping U.S. foreign policy have occurred in the Middle East.

Lesson Vocabulary

collective security   the keeping of international peace and order

deterrence   the policy of making America and its allies so militarily strong that their very strength will discourage, or prevent, any attack

cold war   a period of more than 40 years during which relations between the two superpowers (United States and Soviet Union) were at least tense, and often hostile; a time of threats and military build-up

containment   a policy based in the belief that if communism could be kept within its existing boundaries, it would collapse under the weight of its internal weaknesses

détente   French term meaning "a relaxation of tensions"

Lesson Summary
DIPLOMACY

MODIFIED CORNELL NOTES

The State Department, headed by the secretary of state, is the President's right arm in foreign affairs. International law gives all nations the **right of legation**—the right to send and receive diplomatic representatives. The President appoints **ambassadors** who each represent the nation and head an embassy in a country recognized by the United States. They and other embassy workers have **diplomatic immunity**—they cannot be prosecuted for breaking their host country's laws. The State department issues **passports**, which are needed to enter other countries. A passport is a legal document that identifies a person as a citizen of a certain state. A passport is different from a **visa**, which is needed to enter a foreign country. Visas are issued by the country one intends to enter.

For more than 50 years, a major tool of American foreign policy has been **foreign aid**—economic and military assistance for other nations. Foreign aid is allocated to countries that are the most crucial to meeting the foreign policy objectives of the United States; in recent years, these have been Israel, the Philippines, and Latin American countries. Most economic foreign aid must be used to buy American goods and services, so the program also helps the U.S. economy.

Since World War II, the United States has constructed a network of **regional security alliances**—mutual defense pacts in which the United States and other nations agree to work together to meet aggression in a particular part of the world. For instance, the North Atlantic Treaty Organization, or NATO, promotes the collective defense of Europe. In recent years, NATO has increasingly focused on crisis management and peacekeeping.

(Continues on the next page.)

Lesson Vocabulary

right of legation   the right to send and receive diplomatic representatives

ambassador   an official representative of the United States appointed by the President to represent the nation in matters of diplomacy

diplomatic immunity   when ambassadors are not subject to the laws of the state to which they are accredited

passport   a legal document issued by a state that identifies a person as a citizen of that state and permits travel to and from that state

visa   a permit to enter another country, obtained from the country one wishes to enter

foreign aid   economic and military aid to other countries
regional security alliances   treaties in which the U.S. and other countries involved have agreed to take collective action to meet aggression in a particular part of the world

TOPIC 6 · LESSON 5 — Lesson Summary
DIPLOMACY (continued)

The United States first showed its willingness to act as a world power when, after World War II, it led fifty nations in forming the United Nations (UN). The goal of the UN is world peace. It sends armed peacekeeping forces from member nations to help countries in conflict. The UN also sponsors economic and social programs, works to improve world health and protect the environment, and promotes human rights. It is composed of six major organizations: the General Assembly, the Security Council, the Economic and Social Council, the Trusteeship Council, the International Court of Justice, and the Secretariat. The UN Security Council bears the UN's major responsibility for maintaining international peace. It is made up of fifteen members, five of which are permanent members. The Economic and Social Council is responsible to the Assembly for carrying out the UN's many economic, cultural, educational, health, and related activities. The International Court of Justice, or World Court, is the judicial arm of the UN. The Secretariat is the civil service branch of the UN. The secretary-general heads the Secretariat and a staff of 40,000. He or she plays a major role in negotiating and settling international disputes. The United States has not always agreed with UN policy decisions but works closely with the UN on a number of environmental and humanitarian issues.

TOPIC 6 LESSON 6

Lesson Summary
NATIONAL SECURITY

Congress established the Department of Defense in the National Security Act of 1947. Headed by the secretary of defense, the Department of Defense accounts for about a fifth of all federal spending.

The three branches of the military—the Departments of the Army, Navy, and Air Force—are sub-Cabinet departments within the Department of Defense. The army, which is essentially a ground-based force, is the largest and oldest of the armed services. The navy is responsible for sea warfare. The air force has primary responsibility for military air and aerospace operations.

In addition to the Departments of State and Defense, several government agencies are closely involved with U.S. foreign and defense policy. The Director of National Intelligence (DNI) heads the Office of the Director of National Intelligence and controls the Federal Bureau of Investigation (FBI), the Drug Enforcement Administration (DEA), and the Central Intelligence Agency (CIA). The CIA conducts worldwide intelligence operations through **espionage**, or spying.

The Department of Homeland Security (DHS), created in 2002, is charged with protecting the U.S. against **terrorism**, the use of violence to intimidate a government or society, usually for political or ideological reasons. The DHS bears responsibility for border and transportation security, infrastructure protection, emergency preparedness, chemical, biological, radiological and nuclear defense, and intelligence.

Lesson Vocabulary

espionage spying
terrorism the use of violence to intimidate a government or society

TOPIC 6 — Review Questions
THE EXECUTIVE BRANCH AT WORK

Answer the questions below using the information in the Lesson Summaries on the previous pages.

Lesson 1: The Federal Bureaucracy

1. Who is responsible for overseeing all of the government's many agencies and administrators?

_____

_____

2. Categorize The Office of Management and Budget assists the President in preparing the budget, and NASA is responsible for pioneering the future in space exploration. Categorize each as a staff or line agency, and explain why.

_____

_____

Lesson 2: The EOP and the Executive Departments

3. Describe the relationship that members of the White House Office have with the President.

_____

_____

4. Draw Inferences Why do you think it is important that the President select the executive department heads (the Cabinet)?

_____

_____

Lesson 3: The Independent Agencies

5. Identify Causes and Effects Congress located the independent agencies outside of Cabinet departments. What do you think would happen if the independent agencies were located within Cabinet departments?

_____

_____

6. Determine Central Ideas The Nuclear Regulatory Commission licenses and regulates the use of nuclear energy to protect public health, safety, and the environment. It also sets rules and standards for nuclear reactors, facilities, and waste materials. These are important issues to U.S. citizens. Why is it most effective for this to be handled by a regulatory commission instead of by Congress?

_____

_____

TOPIC 6

Review Questions

THE EXECUTIVE BRANCH AT WORK (continued)

Lesson 4: Foreign Policy Overview

7. Does a nation's foreign policy have to do only with matters of defense? Explain your answer.

_____

_____

8. During the cold war, did the United States pursue a policy of isolationism? Explain your answer.

_____

_____

Lesson 5: Diplomacy

9. Draw Inferences The State Department has been called "the President's right arm in foreign affairs." How do you think the secretary of state helps the President?

_____

_____

10. Assess an Argument Consider the following argument in favor of continued economic aid to other nations and then assess whether the argument is valid: Foreign economic aid to other countries is a good investment for the United States. It comprises only one percent of the entire federal budget, some $20 billion dollars, and yet returns untold amounts in increased sales of American goods and services.

_____

_____

_____

Lesson 6: National Security

11. If the U.S. Navy needed a new warship, which Cabinet department head would most likely make the case to Congress or to the President? Why?

_____

_____

12. Draw Conclusions Department of Homeland Security was created to protect the United States against terrorism. Why do you think this agency is also responsible for U.S. border security?

_____

_____

TOPIC 7

Note Taking Study Guide

THE JUDICIAL BRANCH

Focus Question: How should we handle conflict?

As you read, note the various courts of the U.S. federal judicial system—the branch of government that handles legal conflict.

The Judicial Branch of the Federal Government

COURTS	POWERS, JURISDICTION
Constitutional Courts	• deal with matters involving the "judicial power of the United States" •
Supreme Court	• • •
Courts of appeals	• • do not conduct trials or accept new evidence •
District courts	• conduct federal trials in a total of 94 courts, at least one per State •
Court of International Trade	•
Special Courts	•
Court of Appeals for the Armed Forces	• can review the more serious court-martial convictions of military personnel •
Court of Appeals for Veterans Claims	• • decides appeals regarding veterans' benefits
Court of Federal Claims	•
Tax Court	•
Territorial courts	•

TOPIC 7
LESSON 1

Lesson Summary
THE NATIONAL JUDICIARY

The Constitution creates the Supreme Court and leaves to Congress the creation of the **inferior courts**—those federal courts under the Supreme Court. Congress has created two distinct types of federal courts. Constitutional courts deal with matters involving the "judicial power of the United States." Special courts, such as the U.S. Tax Court, deal with cases related to the expressed powers of Congress. Because the Framers of the Constitution thought it essential that all federal judges be separated from public pressure and coercion of other branches of government, they stipulated that federal judges be appointed rather than elected. The Framers also stipulated that all federal judges serve for life, except for judges that serve in special courts. In addition, it is important to note that the U.S. has a dual-court system: a federal court system, which spans the entire country, and a State court system in each of the fifty States.

Jurisdiction, or the authority to hear federal cases or cases involving admiralty or maritime law, belongs to constitutional courts. Federal courts have exclusive jurisdiction over cases that may only be heard by them. Federal and State courts have **concurrent jurisdiction** over cases that may be tried by either. Such cases may be disputes among residents of different States. In some of these cases, the **plaintiff**, the person filing the case, may choose to bring it to federal or State court. The **defendant**, the person against whom the complaint is made, may be able to have a case moved from a State court to a federal court.

A court that first hears a case has **original jurisdiction** over it. A court that hears a case on appeal from a lower court has **appellate jurisdiction** over the case.

(Continues on the next page.)

Lesson Vocabulary

inferior courts   the lower federal courts, beneath the Supreme Court

jurisdiction   the authority of a court to hear a case

concurrent jurisdiction   power shared by federal and State courts to hear certain cases

plaintiff   in civil law, the party who brings a suit or some other legal action against another (the defendant) in court

defendant   in a civil suit, the person against whom a court action is brought by the plaintiff; in a criminal case, the person charged with the crime

original jurisdiction   the power of a court to hear a case first, before any other court

appellate jurisdiction   the authority of a court to review decisions of inferior (lower) courts

TOPIC 7 LESSON 1

Lesson Summary

THE NATIONAL JUDICIARY (continued)

The President nominates federal judges, and the Senate then confirms them. Judges of the Supreme Court and the constitutional courts serve for life and may only be removed from office by impeachment. Many factors, including senatorial courtesy, prior judicial experience, and political party, affect the selection. Another major determining factor is judicial philosophy. The proponents of **judicial restraint** believe that judges should decide cases on the basis of (1) the original intent of the Framers or those who enacted the statute(s) involved in a case and (2) **precedent**—a judicial decision that serves as a guide for settling later cases of a similar nature. Those who support **judicial activism** take a much broader view of judicial power. They argue that provisions in the Constitution and in statute law should be interpreted and applied in the light of ongoing changes in conditions and values—especially in cases involving civil rights and social welfare issues.

Lesson Vocabulary

judicial restraint   a judicial philosophy in which supporters believe that judges should decide cases based on the original intent of the Framers or those who enacted the statute(s) involved in a case, or on precedent

precedent   a judicial decision that serves as a guide for settling later cases of a similar nature

judicial activism   a judicial philosophy in which supporters believe that judges should interpret and apply provisions in the Constitution and in statute law in light of ongoing changes in conditions and values

Lesson Summary
THE SUPREME COURT

MODIFIED CORNELL NOTES

The Supreme Court is made up of the Chief Justice and eight associate justices. It is the final authority for any case involving questions of federal law. It has the final power of **judicial review**, the power to decide the constitutionality of an act of government. In 1803, the Supreme Court case *Marbury* v. *Madison* established this power.

The Supreme Court has both original and appellate jurisdiction. Most of its cases come on appeal. It hears cases in original jurisdiction when either a State or a diplomat is involved.

The Supreme Court decides only about 100 cases a year. Most reach the Court by writ of certiorari, which is an order to a lower court to send up a case record for review. A few cases reach the Court by **certificate**—that is, a lower court asks the Supreme Court to certify an answer to a matter in its case. At least four of its nine justices must agree that a case should be put on the Court's docket.

When the Court accepts a case, each side sends the Court a **brief**—a detailed written report supporting its side of the case. Both sides then present oral arguments, after which the justices vote on the case. The justices explain their decision in writing with a **majority opinion**, which gives the Court's official position and details the reasons for the majority opinion. Each of these opinions stands as a **precedent**, or an example, for similar cases. A justice who agrees with the decision may write a **concurring opinion** to add points to the majority opinion. A justice who disagrees with the ruling may write a **dissenting opinion**.

Lesson Vocabulary

judicial review   the power of the court to determine if an act of government, whether executive, legislative, or judicial, is constitutional

certificate   the result of a process in which a lower court asks the Court to certify the answer to a specific question, such as a procedure or rule of law

brief   written statement that spells out the party's legal position and cites relevant facts and legal precedents

majority opinion   the opinion on which the decision of the Court is based, which identifies the issues in the case and the reasons for the decision

precedent   an earlier decision that can serve as a guide for a later decision

concurring opinion   an opinion that is basically in agreement with the decision that the Court has made, but which bases that opinion on different reasons

dissenting opinion   an opinion written by a justice who does not agree with the Court's decision, explaining the reasons why not

Lesson Summary
THE INFERIOR COURTS AND THE SPECIAL COURTS

MODIFIED CORNELL NOTES

The inferior courts, the federal courts under the Supreme Court, handle most federal cases. Each State, the District of Columbia, Puerto Rico, the Virgin Islands, Guam, and the Northern Mariana Islands has at least one district court or federal trial court.

The 94 U.S. district courts have original jurisdiction over most federal criminal cases and federal civil cases. A federal **criminal case** is filed when a person violates a federal law. A federal **civil case** involves some noncriminal matter, such as a contract dispute.

When the Supreme Court's **docket**—its list of cases to be heard—grew too long, Congress created the courts of appeals to hear appeals from district courts. The United States now has 13 courts of appeals serving 12 judicial circuits. The Court of Appeals for the Federal Circuit is the thirteenth of these appellate tribunals. It sits in the District of Columbia, but its jurisdiction is nationwide; it is mostly concerned with appeals of decisions in patent, copyright, and international trade cases. Altogether, 179 circuit judges sit on these appellate courts, with a justice of the Supreme Court assigned to each of them. They do not conduct trials or accept new evidence in the cases they hear. Instead, they review the record, the transcript of proceedings made in the trial court, and they ponder the oral and written arguments (the briefs) submitted by attorneys representing parties to a case.

One other Article III, or constitutional, court is the U.S. Court of International Trade, which hears civil cases involving trade-related laws.

The special courts of the U.S. federal court system are also called legislative or Article I courts. Beginning in 1789, Congress created a system of military courts for each branch of the nation's armed forces, as an exercise of its expressed power to "make Rules for the Government and Regulation of the land and naval Forces." These military courts—**courts-martial**—serve the special disciplinary needs of the armed forces and are not a part of the federal court system. In

(Continues on the next page.)

Lesson Vocabulary

criminal case   a case in which a defendant is tried for committing a crime as defined by the law

civil case   a case involving a noncriminal matter such as a contract dispute or a claim of patent infringement

docket   a court's list of cases to be heard

courts-martial   courts composed of military personnel, for the trial of those accused of violating military law

Name _____ Class _____ Date _____

MODIFIED CORNELL NOTES

1950, Congress created the Court of Military Appeals, now titled the Court of Appeals for the Armed Forces, to review the more serious court-martial convictions of military personnel. This appellate court is a **civilian tribunal**, a part of the judicial branch, entirely separate from the military establishment. Two courts hear cases from the military. The Court of Appeals for the Armed Forces is a civilian tribunal, meaning that its judges are civilians. This is the court of last resort for cases involving military law. It may review the decision of a court-martial, or a court composed of military personnel that puts those accused of violating military law on trial. The Court of Appeals for Veterans Claims also hears cases that involve the military. It decides appeals regarding veterans' benefits.

The United States cannot be sued by anyone unless Congress agrees to the case. Congress established the Court of Federal Claims to hear such cases and to allow a citizen to secure **redress**, or satisfaction of the claim, usually through payment. The Tax Court hears civil cases that involve tax law. Most of its cases are generated by the Internal Revenue Service and other agencies of the Treasury Department.

Congress created territorial courts to judge cases in U.S. territories, such as the Virgin Islands. The District of Columbia, which is neither a State nor a territory, also has its own court system.

Lesson Vocabulary

civilian tribunal   a court operating as part of the judicial branch, entirely separate from the military establishment

redress   satisfaction of a claim; payment

TOPIC 7

Review Questions

THE JUDICIAL BRANCH

Answer the questions below using the information in the Lesson Summaries on the previous pages.

Lesson 1: The National Judiciary

1. If residents of two different states had a legal dispute, would it be handled by a federal or a State court?

_____

_____

2. **Compare and Contrast** What is the difference between a court with original jurisdiction and one with appellate jurisdiction?

_____

_____

Lesson 2: The Supreme Court

3. Why is judicial review such an important power for the Supreme Court to have?

_____

_____

4. **Draw Conclusions** For cases heard by the Supreme Court, which do you think is more important, the brief or the oral argument? Why?

_____

_____

Lesson 3: The Inferior Courts and the Special Courts

5. **Identify Supporting Details** What is special about the Court of Appeals for the Federal Circuit?

_____

_____

6. If a company files a civil suit against the Internal Revenue Service, which court would most likely hear the case?

_____

_____

Name _____ Class _____ Date _____

TOPIC 8

Note Taking Study Guide
PROTECTING CIVIL LIBERTIES

Focus Question: How much power should the government have?

As you read, note how government promotes civil rights, and also note the limits on government power as represented by civil liberties.

Civil Rights and Liberties	Legal Protections
Freedom of religion	
Freedom of speech and the press	
No prior restraint	
Freedom of assembly and petition	People are free to gather to share their opinions on public issues; people are free to bring their views to the attention of public officials.
Content neutral rules	
Due process	
Limits on discrimination	
Probable cause	
Exclusionary rule	
No bill of attainder	
No ex post facto law	
Right to a trial	
The 5th Amendment	
Limits on bail	
Punishment	

Name _____ Class _____ Date _____

MODIFIED CORNELL NOTES

The Declaration of Independence states that people have certain unalienable rights, or individual freedoms that are theirs from birth. The first ten amendments to the Constitution, known as the Bill of Rights, list these rights.

The Constitution guarantees Americans both civil liberties and civil rights, terms that are often used interchangeably. However, **civil liberties** are protections against government acts while **civil rights** are positive acts of government that uphold the Constitution.

Each constitutional guarantee of civil liberty limits the power of government. However, Americans do not have total freedom. They may use their freedoms only in ways that do not infringe on the rights of others. Most constitutional rights belong to all people living in the United States, including **aliens**—foreign-born residents or noncitizens.

The Bill of Rights applies only to the National Government. Most of its protections are applied to the State governments by the 14th Amendment's Due Process Clause. This clause states that "No State shall . . . deprive any person of life, liberty, or property, without due process of law." Through a series of cases, the Supreme Court has engaged in the **process of incorporation** by which most of the guarantees in the Bill of Rights have been included in the Due Process Clause.

Lesson Vocabulary

civil liberties   guarantees of the safety of persons, opinions, and property from the arbitrary acts of government, including freedom of speech and freedom of religion

civil rights   term used for positive acts of government that seek to make constitutional guarantees a reality for all people, e.g., prohibitions of discrimination

alien   foreign-born resident, or noncitizen

process of incorporation   the process of incorporating, or including, most of the guarantees in the Bill of Rights into the 14th Amendment's Due Process Clause

TOPIC 8 LESSON 2

Lesson Summary
FREEDOM OF RELIGION

Free expression, including freedom of religion and freedom of the press, is necessary in a free society. The 1st Amendment guarantees religious freedom through its Establishment Clause and its Free Exercise Clause. The 14th Amendment's Due Process Clause protects this freedom from acts of the States.

The Establishment Clause states that "Congress shall make no law respecting an establishment of religion." Thomas Jefferson described the clause as setting up "a wall of separation between church and state." The nature of the "wall," particularly as it applies to education, is not agreed upon and has therefore been the subject of many court cases. For example, in 1925, the Supreme Court ruled that a State government could not force parents to send their children to public schools instead of private, church-related parochial schools. Recent establishment cases have centered on State aid to **parochial** schools. In 1971, the Supreme Court established a three-pronged standard, known as the *Lemon* test, to decide whether a State law amounts to an establishment of religion. That standard states: (1) a law must have a secular, not religious, purpose; (2) it must neither advance nor inhibit religion; and (3) it must not foster an "excessive entanglement" of government and religion. More often than not, the Court has found laws that provide some form of public aid to church-related schools unconstitutional.

In other rulings, the Court has said that public schools may not sponsor religious events. It has not said, however, that individuals may not pray when and as they choose—in schools or in any other place. The Free Exercise Clause states that Congress shall make no law prohibiting the free exercise of religion. It guarantees to each person the right to believe whatever he or she wishes with regard to religion. However, no person may act on behalf of those beliefs exactly as he or she chooses. For example, people may not break laws or harm others while practicing their religion.

Lesson Vocabulary

parochial   church-related, as in a parochial school

Lesson Summary
FREEDOM OF SPEECH AND PRESS

MODIFIED CORNELL NOTES

The guarantees outlined in the 1st and 14th amendments regarding free speech and free press protect a person's right to speak freely and to hear what others have to say. However, no person has the right to libel or slander another. **Libel** is the false and malicious use of printed words. **Slander** is the false and malicious use of spoken words.

Sedition is the crime of attempting to overthrow or disrupt the government by force or violent acts. Seditious speech, or the urging of such conduct, is not protected by the 1st Amendment. The Supreme Court has limited both seditious speech and obscenity.

Symbolic speech, or communicating ideas by conduct, has been protected by the Supreme Court. **Picketing**, or the patrolling of a business site by striking workers, is one such form of protected conduct when it is peaceful. However, even peaceful picketing can be prohibited if it is conducted for an illegal purpose.

While the Constitution allows government to punish some utterances after they are made, it seldom allows the use of **prior restraint**—the curbing by the government of ideas before they have been expressed. The Court has used this general rule on numerous occasions. When the Nixon administration sought an injunction, or court order, to bar the publication of the Pentagon Papers, arguing that national security was at stake and the documents (government property) had been stolen, the Court found that the government had not shown that printing the documents would endanger the nation's security. Thus, the government did not overcome the "heavy presumption" against prior censorship.

The media is also subject to federal regulation. For instance, reporters do not have a constitutional right to keep their sources confidential. However, thirty States have passed shield laws, which give reporters some protection against having to disclose their sources or reveal other confidential information in legal proceedings in those States. Radio and television are subject to more regulation than newspapers because they use the publicly owned airwaves to distribute their materials.

Lesson Vocabulary

libel   false and malicious use of printed words

slander   false and malicious use of spoken words

sedition   crime of attempting to overthrow the government by force or to disrupt its lawful activities by violent acts

symbolic speech   expression by conduct; communicating ideas through facial expressions, with body language, or by carrying a sign or wearing an armband

picketing   patrolling of a business site by striking workers

prior restraint   idea that government cannot curb ideas before they are expressed

TOPIC 8 LESSON 4

Lesson Summary
FREEDOM OF ASSEMBLY AND PETITION

The 1st and 14th amendments guarantee the right of Americans to **assemble**, or gather, to share their opinions on public matters. The people may organize to influence public policy and to tell public officials what they think. They may also do this through **petitions**—advertisements, letters, and demonstrations. Demonstrations, however, must be peaceful. People do not have the right to block streets or close schools. They may not endanger life, property, or public order. **Civil disobedience**—incidents in which people have purposely violated the law, nonviolently, but nonetheless deliberately, as a means of expressing their opposition to some particular law or public policy—has a long history in our country; however, as a general rule, civil disobedience is not protected by the Constitution.

The government may make rules about the time and place of assemblies and about how they are conducted. These rules must be reasonable and **content neutral**—that is, the rules may not be related to what might be said at the demonstrations.

Most demonstrations take place on public property because demonstrators want to get the public's attention. There is no constitutional right to demonstrate on private property; therefore, no one has a constitutional right to hand out political material or ask people to sign petitions there.

The guarantees of freedom of assembly and petition include a **right of association**. That means that the right to be with others to promote political, economic, and social causes is guaranteed.

Lesson Vocabulary

assemble   to gather with one another in order to express views on public matters

petition   the means by which citizens express their right to bring their views to the attention of public officials, including written petitions, letters, lobbying, and marches

civil disobedience   a form of protest in which people deliberately but non-violently violate the law as a means of expressing their opposition to some particular law or public policy

content neutral   the government may not regulate assemblies on the basis of what might be said

right of association   the right to associate with others to promote political, economic, and other social causes

| TOPIC **8**
LESSON 5 | **Lesson Summary**
DUE PROCESS OF LAW |

The 5th Amendment states that the government cannot deprive a person of "life, liberty, or property, without **due process** of law." The 14th Amendment extends this restriction to the States. Due process means the government must act fairly and in accord with established rules—it must use fair procedures. Fair procedures, however, mean little if used to administer unfair laws. **Procedural due process** refers to the *how* of governmental action, or methods the government must use. **Substantive due process** refers to the *what* of governmental action, or policies under which the government must operate.

The States have the power to protect and promote the public health, safety, morals, and general well-being of all the people. This power is called the **police power**, and the States may not use it in violation of due process. When its use conflicts with civil rights protections, the courts must balance the needs of society against individual rights. In a key case of this type, the Supreme Court supported a police officer who ordered a blood test for a suspected drunk driver, even though the officer had no **search warrant**, or court order authorizing a search.

Another aspect of due process relates to the right of **eminent domain**, that is, the power of the government to take private property for public use. However, the government must provide just compensation for any property it takes. This means that the property's owners must get fair market value for the property.

Lesson Vocabulary

due process   concept that holds that the government must act fairly and in accord with established rules in all that it does

procedural due process   concept that holds that the government must employ fair procedures and methods

substantive due process   concept that holds that the government must create fair policies and laws

police power   authority of each State to act to protect and promote the public health, safety, morals, and general welfare of its people

search warrant   court order authorizing a search

eminent domain   power of a government to take private property for public use

Lesson Summary

FREEDOM AND SECURITY OF THE PERSON

MODIFIED CORNELL NOTES

The 13th Amendment was added to the Constitution in 1865 to end slavery and **involuntary servitude,** or forced labor. It covers the conduct of individuals as well as government. The Supreme Court has ruled that the 13th Amendment authorizes Congress to attack racial **discrimination,** that is, bias or unfairness.

The 2nd Amendment protects the right of each State to keep a militia. It does not guarantee the right of individuals to keep and bear arms. The Supreme Court has never found that right to be within the 14th Amendment's Due Process Clause. Each State can therefore create its own limits on the right to keep and bear arms—and all of the States do, in various ways.

The 3rd and 4th amendments guarantee that government cannot disturb people or their homes without good reason. The 3rd Amendment forbids the unlawful quartering of soldiers in private homes—a British practice in colonial days. The 4th Amendment also grew out of colonial practice. It requires that police officers obtain a proper warrant with **probable cause**—a reasonable suspicion of crime, to search for or seize evidence or persons. The 4th Amendment was designed to protect against the use of **writs of assistance**—blanket search warrants that allowed colonial British officers to search private homes.

(Continues on the next page.)

Lesson Vocabulary

involuntary servitude   forced labor

discrimination   bias, unfairness

probable cause   reasonable grounds, a reasonable suspicion of crime

writs of assistance   blanket search warrant with which British custom officials had invaded private homes to search for smuggled goods

MODIFIED CORNELL NOTES

The **exclusionary rule** states that evidence gained by illegal police action, such as searching without a warrant, cannot be used against the person from whom it was seized. Police do not always need a warrant for a search—for example, they can do so if evidence is in "plain view," or if a suspect is in a public area and there is probable cause to believe the person has committed a crime or is about to commit a crime. Finally, the Court has held that an officer needs no warrant to search an automobile, a boat, an airplane, or some other vehicle, when there is probable cause to believe that it is involved in illegal activities—because such a "movable scene of crime" could disappear while a warrant was being sought.

However, what amounts to illegal police action has been curtailed in the aftermath of 9/11. In 2001, Congress passed the USA Patriot Act, which provides for greatly increased governmental powers to combat domestic and international terrorist activities. Its major provisions focus on three broad areas: surveillance and investigation, immigration, and the financing of terrorist groups. Several provisions raise significant civil liberties issues that, over time, will be tested in the courts. Similarly, the National Security Agency has been allowed to conduct wiretapping to monitor the international telephone calls and e-mails of Americans with suspected ties to terrorists.

The most controversial applications of the right of privacy have come in cases that raise this question: To what extent can a State limit a woman's right to an abortion?

Lesson Vocabulary

exclusionary rule   ruling stating that evidence gained as the result of an illegal act by police cannot be used against the person from whom it was seized

TOPIC 8 LESSON 7

Lesson Summary

RIGHTS OF THE ACCUSED

The Constitution offers several guarantees for persons accused of crimes. For one, it grants the right to seek a **writ of habeas corpus**— a court order commanding an officer imprisoning someone to explain why the prisoner should not be released. It also prohibits the passage of a **bill of attainder**, which punishes a person without a trial. Also, Congress and the States may not pass an **ex post facto law**, which makes an act a crime and then punishes someone for committing the act before the law's passage.

A **grand jury** decides if someone can be accused of a serious crime. The prosecutor presents the grand jury with an **indictment**, or a formal complaint against the accused. The grand jury decides whether there is enough evidence for a trial; if not, the charges are dropped. A **presentment** is a formal accusation brought by the grand jury on its own motion, rather than that of the prosecutor. It is rarely used in federal courts. In most states today, a prosecutor brings charges in an **information**—a document in which he or she swears there is enough evidence for a trial.

An accused person may not be exposed to **double jeopardy**, that is, be tried for the same crime more than once. The person has the right to a speedy and public trial by jury with the assistance of counsel (a lawyer). If a defendant waives this right, a **bench trial** is held, meaning a judge alone hears the case.

(Continues on the next page.)

Lesson Vocabulary

writ of habeas corpus   court order that prevents unjust arrests and imprisonments

bill of attainder   legislative act that inflicts punishment without a court trial

ex post facto law   law applied to an act committed before its passage

grand jury   formal device by which a person can be accused of a serious crime

indictment   formal complaint before a grand jury that charges the accused with one or more crimes

presentment   formal accusation brought by the grand jury on its own motion, rather than that of the prosecutor

information   formal charge filed by a prosecutor without the action of a grand jury

double jeopardy   part of the 5th Amendment stating that no person can be put in jeopardy of life or limb twice; once a person has been tried for a crime, he or she cannot be tried again for the same crime

bench trial   trial heard by a judge without a jury

Lesson Summary
RIGHTS OF THE ACCUSED (continued)

The 5th Amendment protects a person from self-incrimination, or being a witness against himself or herself. The Miranda Rule requires police to read a list of rights to a person they arrest and make sure the person understands these rights.

The 8th Amendment offers protections for Americans being punished for crimes. It forbids the setting of excessive or unreasonably high bail. **Bail** is a sum of money that an accused person must pay the court as a guarantee that he or she will appear in court at the proper time. Once paid, the person goes free until the time of the trial. If the defendant does not come to court, he or she does not get the money back.

In 1984, Congress provided for the **preventive detention** of some people accused of committing federal crimes. This means that federal judges may keep accused felons in jail without bail when there is reason to believe that they will commit additional crimes before trial.

The 8th Amendment also forbids cruel and unusual punishment, such as burning at the stake or crucifixion. The Supreme Court has held that **capital punishment**, or the death penalty, is constitutional if applied fairly. To help ensure that the death penalty is fairly applied, many states use a two-stage process in capital cases: first, a trial to determine innocence or guilt, and then for those convicted, a second proceeding to decide if the circumstances justify the death sentence.

Treason is the only crime the Framers specifically defined in the Constitution; they wanted to prevent tyrants from using the charge of treason to punish political opponents. **Treason** can consist of only two things: making war against the United States and aiding the nation's enemies.

Lesson Vocabulary

bail   sum of money that the accused may be required to post (deposit with the court) as a guarantee that he or she will appear in court at the proper time

preventive detention   law that allows federal judges to order that an accused felon be held, without bail, when there is good reason to believe that he or she will commit yet another serious crime before the trial

capital punishment   death penalty

treason   betrayal of one's country; in the Constitution, by "levying war against the United States or offering comfort or aid to its enemies"

TOPIC 8 — Review Questions
PROTECTING CIVIL LIBERTIES

Answer the questions below using the information in the Lesson Summaries on the previous pages.

Lesson 1: The Unalienable Rights

1. What document within the Constitution lists Americans' unalienable rights?

_____

_____

2. Compare and Contrast Compare and contrast *civil liberties* and *civil rights*. What distinctions can be made between the two terms?

_____

_____

Lesson 2: Freedom of Religion

3. Interpret The 1st Amendment's Establishment Clause guarantees the separation of church and state. What does that guarantee mean?

_____

_____

4. Draw Inferences Is it acceptable, according to the Free Exercise Clause, for a person to stand in the middle of a city street and read aloud from the Bible? Why or why not?

_____

_____

Lesson 3: Freedom of Speech and Press

5. In what ways are the rights of free speech and press limited?

_____

_____

6. Determine Central Ideas In what way do shield laws limit government regulation of the media?

_____

_____

Lesson 4: Freedom of Assembly and Petition

7. Determine Central Ideas Why is the right to assemble peaceably important to a democratic society?

_____

_____

8. What is the general goal of people who engage in civil disobedience?

_____

_____

Lesson 5: Due Process of Law

9. Which form of due process, procedural or substantive, refers to established rules or policies that the government must follow?

_____

_____

10. **Draw Inferences** How is the right of eminent domain linked to the right of due process?

_____

_____

Lesson 6: Freedom and Security of the Person

11. What does the exclusionary rule exclude?

_____

_____

12. **Determine Central Ideas** Why has the Supreme Court made it easier for police to search a car than to search a home?

_____

_____

Lesson 7: Rights of the Accused

13. **Determine Central Ideas** How do bills of attainder and ex post facto laws reflect the principle of separation of powers?

_____

_____

14. **Compare and Contrast** How are the grand jury and the writ of habeas corpus similar in the protections that they offer?

_____

_____

TOPIC **9**	**Note Taking Study Guide**
	CITIZENSHIP AND CIVIL RIGHTS

Focus Question: What are the challenges of diversity?

As you read, note how the United States has had to overcome many challenges, both social and political, on the road to achieving a more diverse society.

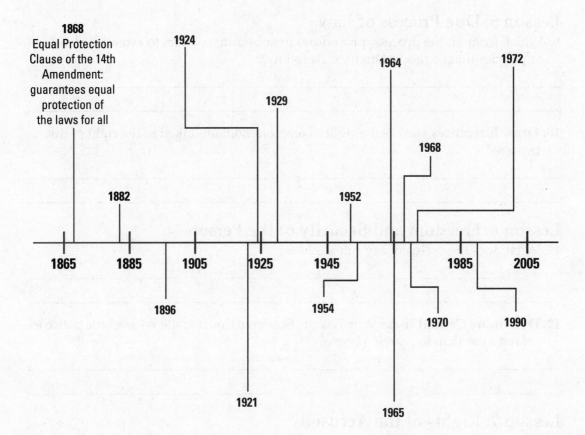

TOPIC 9 LESSON 1

Lesson Summary
AMERICAN CITIZENSHIP

The vast majority of people living in the United States are American **citizens**—people who owe loyalty to the United States and, in turn, receive its protection. Most Americans are citizens because they were born in this country. According to **jus soli,** or the law of the soil, citizenship is determined where one is born. Because of **jus sanguinis,** or the law of the blood, a child born abroad can become an American citizen at birth if he or she is born to a parent who is a U.S. citizen who has lived in the United States at some point in time.

Several million **aliens**—citizens or nationals of a foreign country who live in the United States—become citizens at some point in time after birth through the legal process of **naturalization**, over which Congress has exclusive control. States have no power in the matter.

Americans can choose to give up, or voluntarily abandon, their citizenship. This occurs through the legal process of **expatriation**. Naturalized citizens who have gained citizenship through fraud or deception may lose their citizenship through a court-ordered process called **denaturalization**. A person can neither gain nor lose citizenship by marriage.

Most immigrants to the United States have entered the country officially. At first, immigration into the United States was encouraged. However, by 1890, the frontier was a thing of the past and labor was no longer in short supply. Thus, Congress placed the first restriction on immigration in 1882 with the Chinese Exclusion Act. By the early 1900s, pressure was mounting to limit immigration. Congress responded by adding quantitative limits (numerical ceilings) to the qualitative restrictions (personal characteristics) already in place. The Immigration Acts of 1921 and 1924 and the

(Continues on the next page.)

Lesson Vocabulary

citizen   a member of a state or nation who owes allegiance to it by birth or naturalization and is entitled to full civil rights

jus soli   the law of soil, which determines citizenship based on where a person is born

jus sanguinis   the law of blood, which determines citizenship based on the citizenship of one's parents

alien   a foreign-born resident, or non-citizen

naturalization   the legal process by which citizens of one country become citizens of another

expatriation   the legal process by which a loss of citizenship occurs

denaturalization   the process through which naturalized citizens may involuntarily lose their citizenship

Lesson Summary

AMERICAN CITIZENSHIP (continued)

MODIFIED CORNELL NOTES

National Origins Act of 1929 assigned each country in Europe a quota—a limit on the number of immigrants who could enter the United States from that country each year. In 1952, Congress passed yet another basic law, the Immigration and Nationality Act. This statute modified the quota system, extending it to include every country outside the Western Hemisphere. Congress finally eliminated the country-based quota system in the Immigration and Nationality Act of 1965. Today, the Immigration Act of 1990 governs the admission of aliens to the United States, allowing 675,000 to immigrate into the country each year.

Many others, however, arrive illegally and then face special challenges to stay in this country. Congress has the power to place and remove immigration restrictions. Aliens may be subject to **deportation**, a legal process in which they are required to leave the United States.

Lesson Vocabulary

deportation   a legal process in which aliens are legally required to leave the United States

TOPIC 9 LESSON 2

Lesson Summary
DIVERSITY AND DISCRIMINATION

The United States is a **heterogeneous** society—it is composed of people from different backgrounds. Since the 1960s, the ethnic makeup of the country has changed. Near-record numbers of **immigrants**, or people legally admitted as permanent residents, have helped increase the numbers of African, Asian, and Hispanic Americans.

In our history, white Americans have not been very good at giving an equal place to nonwhite Americans. African, Native, Hispanic, and Asian Americans are four large minority groups that have suffered discrimination from the government and private individuals. African Americans account for about 14 percent of the population. As a group, they have been discriminated against since early colonial days. Native Americans face similar discrimination. Today, more than one-third of the nation's Native American population lives on **reservations**—areas of land reserved for use by Native American tribes. Hispanic Americans make up the largest minority group with a population numbering around 50 million. Many recent Hispanic immigrants have come from Central and South America as **refugees**, or people who leave their homes to seek protection from danger. Asian Americans have faced similar problems assimilating into the white-dominated population. Assimilation is the process by which people of one culture merge into and become part of another culture.

Although not a minority group, women experience discrimination in much the same way that minorities do. They have been treated as less than equal regarding property rights, education, and employment opportunities.

Lesson Vocabulary

heterogeneous   of another or different race, family, or kind; composed of a mix of elements

immigrants   those people legally admitted as permanent residents of a country

reservations   public lands set aside by a government for use by Native American tribes

refugee   one who leaves his or her homeland to seek protection from war, persecution, or some other danger

Name _____ Class _____ Date _____

MODIFIED CORNELL NOTES

The Equal Protection Clause, found in the 14th Amendment, declares that "No State shall…deny to any person within its jurisdiction the equal protection of the laws." Still, the government needs the power to **discriminate**, or treat groups differently. For example, it may treat minors differently than it does adults. However, this power must be limited so that there is equal protection under the law for all Americans. The Supreme Court most often decides equal protection cases by applying a standard known as the **rational basis test**. This test asks: Does the classification in question bear a reasonable relationship to the achievement of some proper governmental purpose? The Court imposes a higher standard in some equal protection cases, however. This is especially true when a case deals with (1) such "fundamental rights" as the right to vote, the right to travel between the States, or 1st Amendment rights; or (2) such "suspect classifications" as those based on race, sex, or national origin. In these instances, the Court has said that a law must meet a higher standard than the rational basis test: the **strict scrutiny test**. A State must be able to show that some "compelling governmental interest" justifies the distinctions it has drawn between classes of people.

Beginning in the late 1800s, many States passed racial **segregation** laws. Segregation is the separation of one group from another. Most of the laws they passed were **Jim Crow laws** that segregated African Americans, meaning they could not share facilities with whites. In 1896, the Supreme Court gave these laws constitutional support with the **separate-but-equal doctrine**.

(Continues on the next page.)

Lesson Vocabulary

discriminate   treat certain categories of people differently than people falling into other categories

rational basis test   test in which the Court asks whether the classification in a law has a reasonable relationship to the achievement of a proper governmental purpose

strict scrutiny test   test in which the Court holds the classification in a law to a higher standard; the State or federal government must show that its law is not related to an ordinary governmental purpose, but to a compelling governmental interest

segregation   separation of one group from another on the basis of race

Jim Crow laws   category of laws that were drafted for the purpose of discriminating against African Americans

separate-but-equal doctrine   doctrine established by the Court in the case *Plessy* v. *Ferguson*, in which it ruled that segregation could be maintained if the separation treated separated races equally

TOPIC
9
LESSON 3

Lesson Summary
EQUALITY BEFORE THE LAW (continued)

In *Plessy* v. *Ferguson*, it ruled that separate facilities of supposed equal quality for whites and African Americans were constitutional.

The Supreme Court began to chip away at the separate-but-equal clause in 1938. However, the Supreme Court has since overturned many of the Jim Crow laws. In 1954, *Brown* v. *Board of Education of Topeka* struck down the separate-but-equal ruling. Then the country made a start toward **integration**—the process of bringing a group into equal membership in society. The Civil Rights Act of 1964 forbade the federal funding of State or local activities that support racial segregation. Finally, in 1970, **de jure segregation**—legally sanctioned segregation—in schools was abolished. However, many communities still have **de facto segregation**—segregation that exists in fact, even if no law requires it—which is often caused by housing patterns.

Gender has long been another basis for unequal treatment. However, since 1971, courts have successfully challenged most laws that allow different treatment of men and women. Finally, despite gay and lesbian rights movements in the 1970s, discrimination on the basis of sexual orientation continues.

Lesson Vocabulary

integration   incorporating people of different races equally into society without separating the races from each other

de jure segregation   segregation in accordance with the law

de facto segregation   segregation as it exists in fact

TOPIC 9
LESSON 4

Lesson Summary

FEDERAL CIVIL RIGHTS LAWS

MODIFIED CORNELL NOTES

From the 1870s to the late 1950s, Congress did not pass any civil rights legislation. Since then, much has been passed. One of the most significant is the Civil Rights Act of 1964. It declares that everyone, regardless of race, color, religion, or national origin, is free to use "public accommodations" such as hotels and restaurants. It also prohibits discrimination—in the workplace and in any program receiving federal funding—based on the reasons above or physical disability, age, or gender. The Civil Rights Act of 1968 prohibits discrimination in the selling or leasing of housing. In Title IX of the Education Amendments of 1972, Congress added a key gender-based guarantee to the provisions of the Civil Rights Act of 1964.

In the 1960s, the Federal Government also began **affirmative action**—a policy requiring employers to take positive steps to remedy the effects of past discrimination. An employer must ensure its workforce reflects the general makeup of the population in its locale and correct inequalities in pay, promotions, and benefits. Rules that call for certain numbers of jobs or promotions to be kept for certain groups are called quotas. Affirmative action applies to all government offices and all businesses that work with the government.

Affirmative action has been criticized for being **reverse discrimination**, or discrimination against the majority group. Supporters and critics of the policy have taken their arguments to the Supreme Court, State legislatures, and the voting booth, where the debate continues. However, recent rulings indicate that the days of affirmative action could be ending.

Lesson Vocabulary

affirmative action a policy of taking active steps to remedy past discrimination

reverse discrimination discrimination against a majority group

TOPIC **9**	**Review Questions**
	CITIZENSHIP AND CIVIL RIGHTS

Answer the questions below using the information in the Lesson Summaries on the previous pages.

Lesson 1: American Citizenship

1. **Determine Central Ideas** In what two ways may a person become a U.S. citizen?

_____

_____

2. **Compare and Contrast** Compare and contrast expatriation and denaturalization.

_____

_____

Lesson 2: Diversity and Discrimination

3. **Identify Causes and Effects** Explain the impact that immigration policies can have on the diversity of the United States.

_____

_____

4. **Draw Conclusions** Which of the four largest minority groups in the United States do you think has faced the most discrimination? Explain your answer.

_____

_____

Lesson 3: Equality Before the Law

5. **Explain an Argument** Do you think restricting voting to citizens aged 18 and over fails the strict scrutiny test for equal protection under the law? Why or why not?

_____

_____

6. **Explain an Argument** How did the case of *Plessy* v. *Ferguson* undermine the Equal Protection Clause of the 14th Amendment?

_____

_____

Lesson 4: Federal Civil Rights Laws

7. The Civil Rights Act of 1964 was linked to federal funding, which would lapse if a State failed to meet the act's requirements. Why was this an effective way of enforcing a law?

_____

_____

8. What federal policy was established in the 1960s to try to correct the effects of past discrimination?

_____

_____

TOPIC 10 Note Taking Study Guide

GOVERNMENT BY THE PEOPLE

Focus Question: What is the role of people in government?

As you read, note the key roles that people play in selecting and influencing their government.

I. Voting

    A. Struggle to extend rights

        1. 1789—only white male property owners

        2. by mid-1800s—

        3. 1870, 15th Amendment—

        4. 1920, 19th Amendment —

        5. 1965—

        6. 1971, 26th Amendment—

    B. Qualifications: three factors

        1.

        2.

        3.

    C. Factors affecting whether and how people vote

        1. Nonvoters—lack feeling that their votes make a difference

        2. Sociological—

        3. Psychological—

    D. Process

        1. By ballot, in person

        2.

II. Public Influences on Public Policy

    A. Public opinion

        1. Factors that influence its development—

        2. Measuring of—

    B. Mass Media

        1. Types—

        2. Role in elections—

        3. Influence—

    C. Interest groups

        1. Role in politics—

        2. Purposes—

        3. Direct approach to government—

        4. Indirect approach to government—

TOPIC 10 LESSON 1 — Lesson Summary
THE HISTORY OF VOTING RIGHTS

Suffrage, also called **franchise**, is the right to vote. In 1789, only white male property owners had this right. Today, the American **electorate**, or the people eligible to vote, includes nearly all citizens who are at least 18 years of age. Two trends caused this change: the elimination of many of the restrictions on suffrage and the shift of power pertaining to suffrage from the States to the Federal Government.

The struggle to extend voting rights began in the early 1800s. Laws were passed to prevent States from restricting suffrage to the extent that they had been. By the mid-1800s, restrictions based on religion and property were eliminated, and nearly all white adult males could vote. In 1870, the 15th Amendment eliminated restrictions based on race; in practice, however, African Americans were still **disenfranchised**, or denied the right to vote, until the passage of several civil rights acts in the 1960s. In 1920, the 19th Amendment added women to the electorate. In 1964, the 24th Amendment dictated that States could not make the payment of a tax a condition for voting. Most recently, in 1971, the 26th Amendment declared that States could not deny anyone 18 or older the right to vote.

In 1870, the 15th Amendment established that the right to vote may not be denied because of race. The amendment was ignored in some southern States, where tactics such as violence, threats, literacy testing, and gerrymandering were used to keep African Americans from voting. **Gerrymandering** is the drawing of electoral district lines in a way that limits a particular group's voting strength.

The civil rights movement pressured Congress to ensure African American voting rights. The Civil Rights Act of 1957 set up the Civil Rights Commission to investigate voter discrimination claims. The Civil Rights Act of 1960 called for federal referees to help all eligible people to register and vote in federal elections. The Civil Rights Act of 1964 emphasized the use of **injunctions**, or orders from the courts

(Continues on the next page.)

Lesson Vocabulary

suffrage   right to vote

franchise   right to vote

electorate   all of the people entitled to vote in a given election

disenfranchised   denied the right to vote

gerrymandering   drawing of electoral district lines to the advantage of a party or group

injunction   court order that forces or limits the performance of some act by a private individual or a public official

TOPIC 10 LESSON 1

Lesson Summary

THE HISTORY OF VOTING RIGHTS (continued)

to do or stop doing something, to ensure that eligible citizens were not kept from voting.

The Voting Rights Act of 1965 made the 15th Amendment truly effective by applying it to all elections—local, State, and federal. It forbade practices that prevented qualified voters from using the polls. Additionally, in those States where a majority of the electorate did not vote in 1964, this act gave the Department of Justice **preclearance**, or the right to approve new election laws, to prevent these laws from weakening minority voting rights. The act was to stay in effect for five years, but it has been extended three times. In 2013, in a monumental and controversial decision, the Supreme Court invalidated the preclearance provision of the Voting Rights Act.

Lesson Vocabulary

preclearance   provision mandated by the Voting Rights Act of 1965 in which no new election laws and no changes in existing election laws, could go into effect in certain States unless first approved by the Department of Justice

TOPIC 10 LESSON 2 — Lesson Summary
YOUR RIGHT TO VOTE

The Constitution's Framers left the power to set suffrage qualifications to the States; they did, however, forbid States from setting different qualifications for who can vote in State and federal elections. Also, State qualifications could not violate any part of the Constitution.

Today, every State requires that any person who wants to vote must be able to satisfy qualifications based on three factors: (1) citizenship, (2) residence, and (3) age. **Aliens**, foreign-born residents who have not become citizens, are generally denied the right to vote in this country. Voters need to be citizens and legal residents of the State in which they wish to vote. In most cases, people must have lived in a State for a certain period of time before they may vote there—a practice meant to give people time to get to know the State's issues as well as prevent outsiders from affecting local elections. Most States also forbid **transients**, or people living in a State for only a short time, from voting there.

There is also an age requirement for voting. In 1971, the 26th Amendment established eighteen as the age at which a State may not deny a person the right to vote.

Forty-nine States—all except North Dakota—require voter **registration**, which is the act of signing up with local election officials. This requirement gives officials lists of registered voters, called **poll books**. State law tells officials to periodically review the poll books and purge them. **Purging** is removing the names of those no longer eligible to vote from the poll books.

Today, no State has a voter requirement of **literacy**—the ability to read or write. Nor does any State require a **poll tax**, a tax paid for voting.

All States deny the right to vote to people in mental institutions or those legally considered mentally incompetent. Most States also deny the right to vote to anyone who has been convicted of a serious crime.

Lesson Vocabulary

aliens   foreign-born residents, or non-citizens

transients   person living in a State for only a short time, without legal residence

registration   procedure of voter identification intended to prevent fraudulent voting

poll books   list of all registered voters in each precinct

purging   process of reviewing lists of registered voters and removing the names of those no longer eligible to vote; a purification

literacy   person's ability to read or write

poll tax   a tax that had to be paid in order to vote

TOPIC 10 LESSON 3

Lesson Summary
VOTING TRENDS

MODIFIED CORNELL NOTES

Millions of Americans who are qualified to vote do not. Voter turnout is low for presidential elections and lower still for **off-year elections**, the congressional elections that are held between presidential elections. In addition, many voters are "nonvoters" who do not vote the entire ballot. As a general rule, the farther down the ballot an office is, the fewer the number of votes that will be cast for it. This phenomenon is sometimes called **ballot fatigue**.

Those who choose not to vote often lack a feeling of **political efficacy**; this means they do not feel that their votes make a difference. They are convinced that "government by the people" has been taken over by politicians, powerful special interest groups, and the media.

Studies of voter behavior focus on the results of particular elections, polls, and **political socialization**—the process by which people gain their political attitudes and opinions. These sources show that certain sociological factors—income, occupation, education, gender, age, religion, ethnicity, region of residence, and family—influence each person's voting choices. For example, there are measurable differences between the electoral choices of men and women, a phenomenon known as the **gender gap**.

Psychological factors—including party identification and perception of the candidates and issues—also contribute to voter behavior. Party identification is loyalty to a political party. A person loyal to one party may vote only for candidates of that party, a practice called **straight-ticket voting**. Recently, many voters have declared themselves **independents**, or people not identified with a party. They may vote for candidates from more than one major party in the same election, which is called **split-ticket voting**.

Lesson Vocabulary

off-year election   congressional election that occurs between presidential election years

ballot fatigue   phenomenon by which voters cast fewer votes for offices listed toward the bottom of the ballot

political efficacy   one's own influence or effectiveness on politics

political socialization   process by which people gain their political attitudes and opinions

gender gap   measurable differences between the partisan choices of men and women today

straight-ticket voting   practice of voting for candidates of only one party in an election

independents   a term used to describe people who have no party affiliation

split-ticket voting   voting for candidates of different parties for different offices in the same election

Lesson Summary
THE VOTING PROCESS

MODIFIED CORNELL NOTES

While the election process is largely governed by State law, federal law regulates the dates and some other aspects of both presidential and congressional elections. For example, Congress sets the date for the national and Congressional elections, requires the use of secret ballots and voting machines, and also acts to protect the right to vote. A **ballot** is the device by which voters register their choices in an election.

Most States hold elections for State offices on the same day Congress has set for national elections: the Tuesday after the first Monday in November of even-numbered years. **Absentee voting**, or voting by those unable to get to their regular polling places, is usually allowed. Some States allow early voting—casting ballots over a period of days before an election. Many argue that State and local elections should not be held on the same day as national elections because of the coattail effect. The **coattail effect** occurs when a strong candidate running for an office at the top of the ballot helps attract voters to other candidates on the party's ticket.

A **precinct** is a voting district. A **polling place**, the place where voters actually vote, is located somewhere in or near a precinct. Most States use a form called the Australian ballot. It is printed at public expense; lists the names of all candidates in an election; is given out only at the polls, one to each voter; and is marked in secret. An office-group ballot lists candidates in a group by office, while a party-column ballot lists them by party.

Well over half the votes now cast in national elections are cast on some type of voting machine—and, increasingly, on some type of electronic voting device. However, one method of casting a ballot—mail-in balloting—does not require any type of voting machine. Instead of going to the polls, voters fill out a ballot at home and mail it back to election officials.

Lesson Vocabulary

ballot   device that voters use to register a choice in an election

absentee voting   provisions made for those unable to go to their regular polling places on election day

coattail effect   effect of a strong candidate running for an office at the top of a ballot, helping to attract voters to other candidates on the party's ticket

precinct   smallest unit of election administration; a voting district

polling place   place where the voters who live in a certain precinct go to vote

MODIFIED CORNELL NOTES

TOPIC 10 LESSON 5

Lesson Summary

PUBLIC OPINION AND POLLING

Public opinion refers to the attitudes of a significant number of people about **public affairs**, or matters of government and politics that concern the people at large. Political socialization is the process by which people learn ideas and develop opinions about issues. Many factors play a part in this process.

Family and education are two of the most important factors in political socialization. Children pick up fundamental attitudes from their families. Schools teach children the value of the American political system and train them to become good citizens.

Other important factors in developing political opinions include occupation and race. Additionally, the mass media—the means of communication that reach many people simultaneously, such as newspapers, television, and the Internet—have a huge impact on the formation of public opinion.

Peer groups are the groups of people with whom one regularly associates, including friends, neighbors, classmates, and co-workers. Members of peer groups usually share political opinions.

Public opinions are also affected by the views expressed by **opinion leaders**—those people who can strongly influence the views of others. Many opinion leaders hold public office. Some commentators, also known as pundits, write for newspapers or magazines, or express their opinions on radio, television, or the Internet. Historic events, such as wars, affect people's lives and thus can also influence public opinion. Government leaders make policy based on public opinion. Of the many ways to measure public opinion, some are more accurate than others.

A winning party and candidate often claim to have a **mandate**, or instructions from the constituency. Based on this, they say that election results indicate public opinion, but few candidates receive

(Continues on the next page.)

Lesson Vocabulary

public opinion   complex collection of the opinions of many different people; the sum of all their views

public affairs   those events and issues that concern the people at large; for example, politics, public issues, and the making of public policies

peer group   people with whom one regularly associates, including friends, classmates, neighbors, and co-workers

opinion leader   any person who, for any reason, has an unusually strong influence on the views of others

mandate   instructions or commands a constituency gives to its elected officials; the term *mandate* comes from the Latin *mandatum*, meaning "a command"

| TOPIC **10** LESSON 5 | ## Lesson Summary
PUBLIC OPINION AND POLLING (continued) |

true mandates. **Interest groups**, or private organizations that work to shape public policy, often present their views as public opinion; however, the exact number of people they represent is unknown. Public officials can use the media and public contacts to gain some sense of public opinion, but it is important to keep in mind that the media are "molders" of public opinion as much as they are "mirrors."

The best measures of public opinion are **public opinion polls**, or devices that collect information through questioning. **Straw votes**, which ask the same question to many people, are not reliable because those who respond may not represent the total population.

Scientific polling, which can be very accurate, breaks the polling process into steps. First, define the universe, that is, the population the poll aims to measure. Then get a **sample**—a representative slice of the universe. Most pollsters will draw a **random sample**, or one in which members of the chosen universe are equally likely to be picked. Some polls use the less reliable quota sample, one that deliberately reflects several of the major characteristics of a given universe. Next, pollsters prepare valid questions, select and control the polling process, and report the results.

Lesson Vocabulary

interest groups private organizations whose members share certain views and work to shape public policy

public opinion poll device that attempts to collect information by asking people questions; *poll* comes from the old Teutonic word *polle*, meaning "the top or crown of the head," the part that shows when heads are counted

straw vote poll that seeks to read the public's mind by asking the same question of a large number of people; the odd name comes from the fact that a straw, thrown up in the air, will indicate which way the wind is blowing

sample representative slice of the public

random sample certain number of randomly selected people who live in a certain number of randomly selected places

TOPIC **10** LESSON 6	**Lesson Summary**
	INFLUENCING PUBLIC OPINION: THE MASS MEDIA

A **medium** is a means of communication; *media* is the word's plural. The American public gets information about public issues through several forms of mass media.

Five major mass media are particularly important in American politics. Television has the most influence, followed by the Internet, newspapers, radio, and magazines. Other media, such as books, also have an impact. The Internet has dramatically altered the way Americans acquire news, and that transformation has been taken a step further by social networking sites. Social media networks have become important tools for fundraising, mobilizing supporters, and uniting political activists worldwide.

The media play a large part in setting the **public agenda**, or the public issues that people think and talk about. In the nineteenth century, most communities had several newspapers, each representing a different partisan perspective. This so-called "partisan press" was based on the loyalty of large numbers of engaged citizens to their political parties—and to their papers. But as news became more nationalized in the early part of the twentieth century, the partisan press disappeared. In the last decade or so, however, the partisan press, including conservative talk radio, partisan Internet news sites, and nontraditional cable television news channels, has reemerged.

The media also have a central role in elections. For example, television has reduced the importance of political parties. In the past, candidates relied on their party members to reach the voters. Now, because television allows the candidates to reach the public directly, many candidates operate with only loose ties to a party. They work hard to get good media coverage and to provide the media with good **sound bites**—focused, snappy statements that can be aired in 35 or 45 seconds.

The influence of the media is limited in some ways. Few people actually follow political issues carefully in the media. Also, those who do tend to watch, listen to, or read their favorite sources rather than sources with contrary opinions to their own. For example, many Democrats do not watch the televised campaign appearances of Republican candidates and vice versa.

Lesson Vocabulary

medium   means of communication; something that transmits information

public agenda   public issues on which the people's attention is focused

sound bite   short, sharply focused report that can be aired in 35 or 45 seconds

TOPIC 10 LESSON 7
Lesson Summary
UNDERSTANDING INTEREST GROUPS

An **interest group** is a private organization whose members share similar views. It tries to promote its interests by influencing **public policy**, or the goals a government sets and the actions it takes to meet them. Interest groups work at the federal, State, and local levels.

Interest groups and political parties both exist for political purposes; however, the goals of interest groups and political parties are different. Political parties care mostly about *who* takes part in government, while interest groups care mostly about *what* the government does—especially pertaining to certain issues.

The role of interest groups in politics is controversial. In their favor, they stimulate interest in **public affairs**, or issues that concern the people at large. They offer people a chance to participate in politics and find others who may not live near them, but who share their views. They often provide useful information to the government, while also keeping close tabs on it. Since they compete with one another, interest groups often limit each other's extremes.

Interest groups are criticized for having more influence than they deserve based on the worth of their causes or the number of people they represent. It can be hard to tell how many people an interest group represents. Some interest groups do not represent the views of all the people for whom they claim to speak. Finally, some interest groups do engage in dishonest behavior.

Many Americans belong to several organizations that meet the definition of an interest group. Such groups may be very large or quite small. Most interest groups represent economic—that is, income-earning—interests, such as business, labor, and agriculture. A trade association is an interest group formed by one segment of the business community, such as banking. A **labor union** is an interest group whose members are workers who hold similar jobs or work in the same industry, such as police officers.

(Continues on the next page.)

Lesson Vocabulary

interest group   private organization whose members share certain views and work to shape public policy

public policy   all of the many goals that a government pursues in all of the many areas of human affairs in which it is involved

public affairs   those events and issues that concern the people at large; for example, politics, public issues, and the making of public policies

labor union   organization of workers who share the same type of job, or who work in the same industry, and press for government policies that will benefit its members

TOPIC 10

LESSON 7

Lesson Summary
UNDERSTANDING INTEREST GROUPS (continued)

MODIFIED CORNELL NOTES

Interest groups reach out to the public for three purposes. First, they supply the public with information in an effort to gain support for their causes. Second, they work to build a positive image for their group. Third, they promote the public policies they favor.

To achieve their goals, interest groups approach the government directly and indirectly. The direct approach is referred to as lobbying. **Lobbying** is the process by which organized interests attempt to affect the decisions and actions of public officials. **Lobbyists** are those people who try to persuade public officials to do those things that interest groups want them to do. Every important interest and many lesser ones—business groups, labor unions, farm organizations, professional associations, churches, veterans, environmental groups, and many more—maintain lobbyists in Washington. Lobbyists make campaign contributions, provide information, write speeches, and even draft legislation. Lobbyists reach out to executive aides and use the courts to achieve their policy goals. For some, like the American Civil Liberties Union, legal action is the primary means by which they seek to influence public policy. An interest group may also file an **amicus curiae** ("friend of the court") **brief** in a case to which it is not itself a party but in which it does have a stake.

Interest groups also use indirect approaches, including **grass-roots pressures**, or organized pressure from citizens at large. Letter writing, demonstrations, and protest marches are all forms of grass-roots lobbying. Interest groups also often use **propaganda**—a technique of persuasion aimed at influencing individual or group behaviors to create certain beliefs. These beliefs may be true, false, or partly true.

Interest groups recognize the role of political parties in selecting policy makers; they try to influence political parties to get policy makers elected who favor their position. Some interest groups form political action committees (PACs) to raise campaign funds for candidates whom they think will further their goals.

Lesson Vocabulary

lobbying   activities by which group pressures are brought to bear on legislators, the legislative process, and all aspects of the public policymaking process

lobbyist   person who tries to persuade public officials to do those things that interest groups want them to do

amicus curiae brief   legal Latin term meaning "friend of the court"; a document that consists of written arguments presented to a court in support of one side in a dispute

grass-roots pressures   pressures on public officials from members of an interest group or the people at large

propaganda   a technique of persuasion aimed at influencing individual or group behaviors to create certain beliefs

TOPIC 10 Review Questions
GOVERNMENT BY THE PEOPLE

Answer the questions below using the information in the Lesson Summaries on the previous pages.

Lesson 1: The History of Voting Rights

1. Draw Conclusions Why do you think suffrage in 1789 was limited to white male property owners?

_____

_____

_____

2. Vocabulary: Determine Meanings Explain the meaning and intended purpose of preclearance.

_____

_____

_____

Lesson 2: Your Right to Vote

3. Why do States and not the Federal Government set the qualifications for voting?

_____

_____

4. What are the three main qualifications for voting in elections?

_____

_____

Lesson 3: Voting Trends

5. Identify Main Ideas What is meant by "off-year elections"? Compare voter turnout in off-year elections with that of elections in other years.

_____

_____

6. Compare and Contrast What are some arguments for and against voting according to party identification, or party loyalty?

_____

_____

Lesson 4: The Voting Process

7. Draw Conclusions Why do you think voting is done by secret ballot and not publicly?

_____

_____

TOPIC 10	**Review Questions**
	GOVERNMENT BY THE PEOPLE (continued)

8. Compare and Contrast How is the effect of straight-ticket voting similar to the coattail effect?

_____

_____

Lesson 5: Public Opinion and Polling

9. Analyze Interactions Who do you think has a stronger effect on political attitudes and actions—one's peer group or opinion leaders?

_____

_____

10. List the steps involved in scientific polling.

_____

_____

Lesson 6: Influencing Public Opinion: The Mass Media

11. Compare and Contrast How do you think the advent of television changed how candidates ran their political campaigns? Similarly, how has the advent of the Internet changed how candidates run their campaigns today?

_____

_____

12. Determine Central Ideas Why are the media able to play a large role in setting the public agenda?

_____

_____

Lesson 7: Understanding Interest Groups

13. Vocabulary: Use Context Clues Use context clues in the text to explain why interest groups are also known as pressure groups.

_____

_____

14. Draw Inferences Why do you think some people have called for restricting the activities of lobbyists?

_____

_____

TOPIC
11

Note Taking Study Guide

ELECTIONS

Focus Question: Who gets elected?

As you read, note what candidates must do to have a chance of getting elected President.

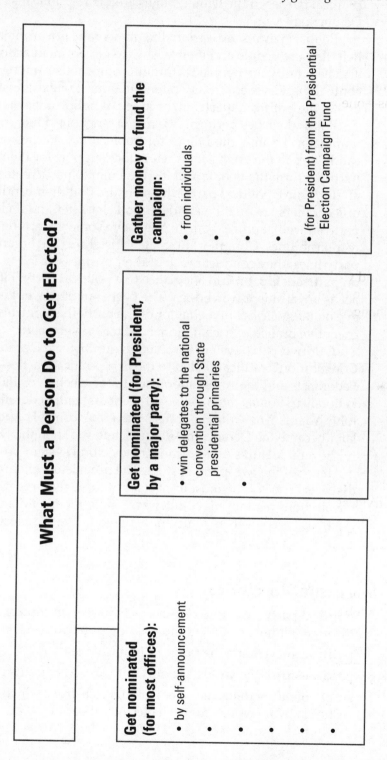

What Must a Person Do to Get Elected?

Gather money to fund the campaign:
- from individuals
- •
- •
- •
- (for President) from the Presidential Election Campaign Fund

Get nominated (for President, by a major party):
- win delegates to the national convention through State presidential primaries
- •

Get nominated (for most offices):
- by self-announcement
- •   •   •   •   •   •

MODIFIED CORNELL NOTES

A **political party** is a group of people who try to control government by winning elections and holding public offices. The two major political parties in the United States are the Republicans and the Democrats.

Political parties are essential to democratic government. Parties help link the people and their wishes to government action. Parties also help unify the people by finding compromise among contending views and thus, soften the impact of extremists at either end of the **political spectrum**, or range of political views.

Political parties perform five major functions. First, they nominate, or name, candidates for public office. Parties present these candidates to the voters and then gather support for them. Second, parties inform the people and inspire them to participate in public affairs. Third, political parties help ensure that their candidates and officeholders are qualified and of good character and if elected, perform well in office. Fourth, they have some governing responsibilities. Congress and State legislatures are organized along party lines; they conduct much of their business based on **partisanship**, or firm allegiance to a political party. Fifth, parties act as government watchdogs. The party out of power keeps a close eye on the policies and behavior of the party that controls the executive branch of each national or State government.

Our two-party system is rooted in our history. Debate over the Constitution's ratification led to the first political parties—the Federalists and the Anti-Federalists. In the election of 1800, Anti-Federalist Thomas Jefferson beat the incumbent, Federalist President John Adams. The Anti-Federalists then took control of politics. They later became the Democratic-Republicans and then the Democrats.

Several features of the American electoral system promote the existence of the two-party system. The prevalence of **single-member districts** is one of the most important of these features. Nearly all of the elections held in this country are single-member district elections, or contests in which only one candidate is elected to each

(Continues on the next page.)

Lesson Vocabulary

political party   a group of persons who seek to control government through winning elections and holding public office

political spectrum   the range of political views

partisanship   the strong support of their party and its policy stands

single-member districts   electoral districts from which one person is chosen by the voters for each elected office

TOPIC 11 LESSON 1 — Lesson Summary
POLITICAL PARTIES AND WHAT THEY DO (continued)

office on the ballot. The winning candidate is the one who receives a **plurality**, or the largest number of votes cast for the office. The two major parties act in a **bipartisan** way to find common ground and shape election laws that discourage non-major-party candidates. Also, while not all Americans are alike, there is a broad **consensus**— a general agreement among various groups—on matters of fundamental importance. This has often resulted in two major parties that often seem a lot alike.

Some critics of the two-party system say that a multiparty system would provide for a broader representation of the electorate and be more responsive to the will of the people. However, one weakness of a multiparty system is that one party is often unable to win the support of a majority of the voters. As a result, the power to govern must be shared by a number of parties in a **coalition**, or temporary alliance of several groups who come together to form a working majority to control a government.

There are four distinct types of minor parties in the United States. **Ideological parties** are those based on a particular set of beliefs—a comprehensive view of social, economic, and political matters. Although long-lived, they seldom are able to win many votes. **Single-issue parties** focus on one public policy matter. They fade away after the issue has been resolved, or people lose interest. Sometimes they are able to get one of the major parties to take on their issue. **Economic protest** parties appear during tough financial times. They criticize the economic actions and plans of the major parties. Most of the important minor parties in American politics have been **splinter parties**—parties that have broken away from one

(Continues on the next page.)

Lesson Vocabulary

plurality   the largest number of votes cast for the office

bipartisan   supported by two parties

consensus   a general agreement among various groups

coalition   a temporary alliance of several groups who come together to form a working majority and so to control a government

ideological parties   parties based on a particular set of beliefs—a comprehensive view of social, economic, and political matters

single-issue parties   parties that focus on a single public question

economic protest   parties rooted in poor economic times, lacking a clear ideological base, dissatisfied with current economic conditions and demanding better times

splinter parties   parties that have split away from one of the major parties

MODIFIED CORNELL NOTES

of the major parties. Usually they have a strong leader who did not win a major party's nomination. Although most Americans do not support them, minor parties still have an impact on politics and on the major parties. The minor parties act as critics and innovators, drawing attention to controversial issues. Strong third-party candidates can also play the "spoiler" role in elections. This means that they pull votes away from one of the major parties, weakening that party's ability to win an election.

The two major parties are highly decentralized. The President's party automatically has a leader, but the other party does not have anyone comparable. The decentralized nature of the parties is in large part a result of the nominating process, which pits party member against party member.

At the national level, both major parties are composed of several basic elements. They are structured around a national convention, a national committee, and two congressional campaign committees. The primary function of the national convention is picking the party's presidential and vice-presidential nominees. Campaign committees in each house of Congress work to reelect incumbents and to make sure that "open seats" remain in the party.

At the State and local levels, State law largely determines party structure. As is the case at the national level, the party is decentralized and built around a State central committee whose members represent major geographic regions in the State. Party structure follows the electoral map of the State, with a party unit for each of the following districts in which elective offices are to be filled: congressional and legislative districts, counties, cities and towns, wards, and precincts. **Wards** are the units into which cities are divided for the election of city council members. **Precincts** are the smallest unit of election administration.

Lesson Vocabulary

wards   a unit into which cities are often divided for the election of city council members

precincts   the smallest unit of election administration; the voters in each precinct cast their ballots at one polling place located within the precinct

Lesson Summary
NOMINATIONS

MODIFIED CORNELL NOTES

Nomination—the process of naming candidates who will seek office—is a critical step in the American democratic system. It precedes the general election, when voters select the officeholders.

In the United States, nominations are made in one the following five ways: (1) self-announcement, a person who wants to run for office simply announces the fact; (2) **caucus**, a group of like-minded people nominate a candidate; (3) at a convention, or a meeting of the party's members; (4) direct primary; and (5) petition.

Most States now nominate candidates through a **direct primary**—an election held within a party to pick its candidates—of which there are multiple kinds. In **closed primaries**, generally only registered party members may vote. In **open primaries**, any voter may vote in one party's primary. Until 2000, when it was ruled unconstitutional, three States used a **blanket primary**, in which voters could choose among all contenders, regardless of party. In some States, a candidate must get more than half the votes to win a primary. If no candidate succeeds, the two top vote-getters hold a **runoff primary** to determine the winner. In most States, nearly all elected school and municipal offices are filled through **nonpartisan elections**, in which candidates are not identified by party. Also common is nomination by petition, by which a candidate gets a certain number of qualified voters to sign a petition. Nomination by petition is found most widely at the local level, chiefly for nonpartisan school posts and municipal offices in medium-sized and smaller communities.

Lesson Vocabulary

nomination the process of candidate selection in an electoral system

caucus as a nominating device, a group of like-minded people who meet to select the candidates they will support in an upcoming election

direct primary an election held within a party to pick that party's candidates for the general election

closed primary a party nominating election in which only declared party members can vote

open primary a party-nominating election in which any qualified voter can take part

blanket primary a voting process in which voters receive a long ballot containing the names of all contenders, regardless of party, and can vote however they choose

runoff primary a primary in which the top two vote-getters in the first direct primary face one another

nonpartisan elections elections in which candidates are not identified by party labels

MODIFIED CORNELL NOTES

TOPIC
11
LESSON 3

Lesson Summary
ELECTING THE PRESIDENT

To nominate candidates for President and Vice President, each political party holds a national convention—a meeting at which party delegates vote. Many States use **presidential primaries**, or party elections, to help decide which delegates will go to the national conventions. The rules about primaries vary by State law. In some State primaries, voters choose convention delegates directly. In others, voters choose from among their party's candidates, and the results are used to help select delegates. The timing of the presidential primaries affects the outcome insofar as the primary schedule determines the length of the election season.

A few States allow **winner-take-all contests**. That means that the winner of the primary gains the votes of all State delegates at the convention. The Democratic Party no longer allows such contests. Instead, it uses a complex system of **proportional representation** that gives each candidate that wins at least 15 percent of the primary vote a share of delegate votes. This has resulted in more than half the States holding preference primaries and then picking the delegates themselves at conventions.

Presidential primaries tend to democratize the delegate-selection process. They force would-be nominees to test their candidacies in actual political combat, but for the party out of power, the primaries are often "knock-down, drag-out" affairs. In those States that do not hold presidential primaries, delegates to the national conventions are selected in a system of local caucuses and district and/or State conventions. A **caucus** is a closed meeting of members of a political party who gather to select delegates to the national convention.

(Continues on the next page.)

Lesson Vocabulary

presidential primary   an election in which the party's voters 1) choose State party organization's delegates to their party's national convention, and/or 2) express a preference for their party's presidential nomination

winner-take-all contests   an almost obsolete system whereby a presidential aspirant who won the preference vote in a primary automatically won all the delegates chosen in the primary

proportional representation   rule applied in Democratic primaries whereby any candidate who wins at least fifteen percent of the votes gets the number of State Democratic convention delegates based on his or her share of that primary vote

caucus   as a nominating device, a group of like-minded people who meet to select the candidates they will support in an upcoming election

Lesson Summary
ELECTING THE PRESIDENT (continued)

At the national conventions, each party adopts a **platform**, or statement of its principles and objectives. The party delegates also vote for presidential and vice-presidential candidates. A stirring moment at every convention is the **keynote address**, an opening speech glorifying the party and its leaders.

The campaigns of both parties focus much of their efforts on **swing voters**—the roughly one third of the electorate who have not made up their minds at the start of the campaign and are open to persuasion by either side. They also target the **battleground States**—those States in which the outcome is "too close to call" and either candidate could win. The presidential campaign ends on election day, which is held every four years on the first Tuesday after the first Monday in November. However, the President is not formally elected until the presidential electors' votes are cast and counted, several weeks later.

When the electorate—the voters—vote for President, they are really voting for electors pledged to support a particular candidate. In 48 States, the candidate with the most votes from the electorate, or popular votes, wins all of the State's electoral votes. Maine and Nebraska use a district system to allot electoral votes. Congress counts the electoral votes and declares a winner. If no candidate receives a majority of the votes, the House of Representatives elects the President.

The electoral college system has three problems. First, it is possible for the winner of the popular vote not to become President. If a candidate wins in a State by only a small majority, he or she still gets all its electoral votes. Also, the electoral votes are not divided according to State population and voter distribution. Second, nothing forces a State's electors to vote for the candidate who wins the State's popular vote. Third, a strong third-party candidate could win enough votes to prevent any candidate from winning a majority, thus putting the election into the House.

(Continues on the next page.)

Lesson Vocabulary

platform   a political party's formal statement of basic principles, stands on major issues, and objectives

keynote address   speech given at a party convention to set the tone for the convention and the campaign to come

swing voters   members of the electorate who have not made up their minds at the start of the campaign and are open to persuasion by either side

battleground States   States in which the outcome of an election is too close to call and either candidate could win

Lesson Summary
ELECTING THE PRESIDENT (continued)

Reformers have suggested four methods of changing the electoral system: the **district plan**, the **proportional plan**, the direct popular election, and the national bonus plan. Another quite different approach to electoral college reform has recently surfaced: the **national popular vote plan**—in effect, a proposal to bring about the direct popular election of the President without making any change to the words of the Constitution.

Lesson Vocabulary

district plan   proposal for choosing presidential electors by which two electors would be selected in each State according to the Statewide popular vote and the other electors would be selected separately in each of the State's congressional districts

proportional plan   proposal by which each presidential candidate would receive the same share of a State's electoral vote as he or she received in the State's popular vote

national popular vote plan   proposal for electing the President whereby each State's election laws would provide for all of the State's electoral votes to be awarded to the winner of the national popular vote and enter into an interstate compact agreeing to elect the President by national popular vote

TOPIC 11 — LESSON 4

Lesson Summary

MONEY AND ELECTIONS

Money plays a key role in politics, but it presents serious problems to democratic governments. The amount of money spent in races varies, but presidential campaigns collect and spend the most.

Parties and their candidates draw their money from two basic sources: private contributors and the public treasury. Most campaign money comes from private sources, including individuals, families, candidates themselves, and **political action committees** (PACs). PACs are the political arms of special-interest groups. Presidential candidates receive public **subsidies**, which are grants of money from federal or State treasuries.

Congress has passed several laws to regulate the use of money in presidential and congressional campaigns. Today, these regulations are found in four detailed laws: the Federal Election Campaign Act of 1971 (FECA), the FECA Amendments of 1974 and of 1976, and the Bipartisan Campaign Reform Act of 2002 (BCRA). The 2002 law attempted to close the "soft money" loophole in the 1974 and 1976 statutes; it was upheld in *McConnell* v. *FEC* in 2003. Soft money is money given to State and local party organizations for such "party-building activities" as voter registration or party mailings and advertisements.

The Federal Election Commission (FEC) administers all federal campaign laws. These laws apply mostly to presidential elections and (1) require the timely disclosure of campaign finance data, (2) place limits on campaign contributions, (3) place limits on campaign expenditures, and (4) provide public financing for several parts of the presidential election process. **Super PACs** are independent political action committees, unaffiliated with any political party. Unlike traditional PACs, Super PACs are allowed to raise and spend unlimited amounts, although they must reveal their donors and cannot work directly with a candidate's campaign. The Revenue Act of 1971 created the Presidential Election Campaign Fund. Every person who files a federal income tax return can "check off " (assign) three dollars of his or her tax bill to the fund.

(Continues on the next page.)

Lesson Vocabulary

political action committees   (PACs) political arms of special-interest groups and other organizations with a stake in electoral politics

subsidy a grant, usually from a government to help an organization

Super PACs   independent political action committees, unaffiliated with any political party, which are allowed to raise and spend unlimited amounts; they must reveal their donors and cannot work directly with a candidate's campaign independent political action committees

TOPIC **11** LESSON 4	**Lesson Summary**
	MONEY AND ELECTIONS (continued)

MODIFIED CORNELL NOTES

Loopholes in campaign finance laws allow candidates to avoid some rules. Since the 1970s, federal law has placed limits on **hard money**—that is, contributions that are given directly to candidates for their campaigns for Congress or the White House, are limited in amount, and must be reported. But this led both major parties to exploit the soft-money loophole. Also, a great deal of funds now flow to **527 organizations** (groups not aligned with a political party but interested in certain candidates and policies), which are allowed to raise unlimited sums of money.

Lesson Vocabulary

hard money contributions that are given directly to candidates for their campaigns, are limited, and must be reported to the government

527 organizations political advocacy groups filed in accordance with Section 527 of the Internal Revenue Code, which are not aligned with a political party but try to influence political policies, and are allowed to raise unlimited sums of money

TOPIC 11 Review Questions
ELECTIONS

Answer the questions below using the information in the Lesson Summaries on the previous pages.

Lesson 1: Political Parties and What They Do

1. **Identify Details** Why is it said that political parties are essential to democratic government?

_____

_____

2. What is the main purpose of the national conventions held by the two major political parties?

_____

_____

Lesson 2: Nominations

3. **Draw Inferences** An open primary is also known as a crossover primary. Why is that an appropriate name for this type of nominating election?

_____

_____

4. **Compare and Contrast** Which type of primary gives voters the most choice? Explain your answer.

_____

_____

Lesson 3: Electing the President

5. **Determine Central Ideas** How do presidential primaries serve to test the electability of a candidate?

_____

_____

6. Under the proposed national popular vote plan, how would the winner of the presidential election be chosen?

_____

_____

Lesson 4: Money and Elections

7. Political candidates need money. Why don't they establish their own Super PACs?

_____

_____

8. **Compare and Contrast** How does "hard money" differ from "soft money"?

_____

_____

TOPIC 12

Note Taking Study Guide

GOVERNMENT AND THE ECONOMY

Focus Question: What is the proper role of government in the economy?

As you read, note the various ways that the government is involved in the economy and also note the effects of that involvement.

Government Involvement in the Economy

Economic Policy		Effects
Fiscal policy (Federal Government)	Levy taxes	• Tax increases—take money out of people's pockets and can slow economic growth • Tax cuts—
	Spend money	• Spending increases— • Spending cuts— • When spending exceeds revenue—
Monetary policy (Federal Reserve System)	Control money supply	• Interest rate increase— • Interest rate cut—
	Control availability of credit	• Discount rate increase— • Discount rate cut—
Globalization	Pursue global trade	• •
	Participate in global organizations	• • Allows U.S. to play a role in setting rules for international commerce

TOPIC 12 — LESSON 1

Lesson Summary
TYPES OF ECONOMIC SYSTEMS

Capitalism is an economic system in which individuals are free to own the means of production and maximize profit. In any economy, the basic resources used to make all goods and services—land, labor, and capital—are called **factors of production**. Land includes all natural resources. Capital is all the human-made resources used to produce goods and services. Labor refers to the people who do an economy's work. A capitalist is a person who owns capital and puts it to productive use. An **entrepreneur** is a person who combines land, labor, and capital resources to produce goods or offer services and is willing to risk losses and failure.

Capitalism is a **free enterprise system**—an economic system with private or corporate ownership of and investment in capital goods. To thrive, capitalism needs a **free market**, or a market in which buyers and sellers can buy and sell as they wish. Private ownership, individual initiative, profit, and competition are also required. Under competitive conditions, the **law of supply and demand** determines prices. This law states that when supplies become more plentiful, prices tend to fall; when supplies become scarcer, prices tend to rise. Likewise, prices generally fall when demand drops; when demand increases, prices generally rise. But competition does not always work smoothly. Sometimes one company drives its rivals out of business and becomes a **monopoly**—the only source of a product or service. A trust is a monopoly in which several corporations in the same industry combine to eliminate competition and regulate prices.

(Continues on the next page.)

Lesson Vocabulary

capitalism   economic system in which individuals are free to own the means of production and maximize profits

factors of production   basic resources that are used to make all goods and services

entrepreneur   individual with the drive and ambition to combine land, labor, and capital resources to produce goods or offer services

free enterprise system   economic system characterized by private or corporate ownership of capital goods; investments that are determined by private decisions rather than by state control and determined in a free market

free market   market in which buyers and sellers are free to buy and sell as they wish

law of supply and demand   law stating that when supplies of goods and services become plentiful, prices tend to drop; when supplies become scarcer, prices tend to rise

monopoly   firm that is the only source of a product or service

Name _____ Class _____ Date _____

MODIFIED CORNELL NOTES

Even though **laissez-faire theory** holds that government should play a limited, hands-off role in society, the U.S. government acts to curb monopolies and trusts. Thus, the United States is said to have a mixed economy—one in which private enterprise coexists with some governmental regulation of the economy.

Other economic systems seek to distribute wealth more evenly. Karl Marx, a German philosopher and economist, believed the capitalistic system was unfair. He sought to establish a classless society where all people owned goods in common. Marx had many followers. Some believed that the changes Marx advocated could come about by peaceful, democratic means; they espoused socialism. Others believed that a fair society could only come about as result of a violent revolution or class struggle. These strict Marxists, or communists, advocated for communism.

Socialist governments try to place key industries—utilities, transportation, and steel production—under government control. They also aim to guarantee the public welfare by equally distributing such necessities and services as retirement pensions, universal healthcare, and free university education. This leads to high taxes. Although socialism is waning in Europe, it is growing in developing countries where political leaders can gain control by promising to nationalize major industries that were previously owned by foreign countries.

The first true communist country was Russia. Josef Stalin, Russia's totalitarian leader, demanded **collectivization**, or state ownership of agriculture, and faster production of chemicals, petroleum, and steel. This led to rapid industrial advances, but scarce consumer goods. By the late 1980s, the Soviet Union was dismantling and many state-owned companies underwent **privatization**, the process of returning nationalized enterprises to private ownership. Very few communist economies exist today.

Lesson Vocabulary

laissez-faire theory   theory suggesting that government should play a very limited role in society

collectivization   collective or state ownership of the means of production

privatization   process of returning national enterprises to private ownership

TOPIC 12 LESSON 2

Lesson Summary

FISCAL AND MONETARY POLICY

Besides fostering competition and entrepreneurship, the Federal Government regulates economic activities with the goal of ensuring fairness in the market. It does this via independent agencies within the executive branch. One such agency, the Federal Reserve System or the "Fed," is the central bank in the Unites States. It manipulates the interest rate to expand or contract the amount of money in the economy. The Securities and Exchange Commission (SEC) oversees the country's stock market and ensures that corporations are truthful in all disclosures and do not engage in insider trading. The Department of Labor works through agencies such as the Occupational Safety and Health Administration (OSHA) to guarantee workers fair and safe workplaces.

The **gross domestic product (GDP)**, or total value of all goods and services produced in the United States each year, now exceeds $15 trillion. While corporations play a huge part in the economy, the Federal Government also plays a part as it seeks to achieve full employment, price stability, and economic growth. Full employment exists when there are enough jobs for people who want them. Price stability refers to the absence of significant ups and downs in prices. A general increase in prices throughout the economy is **inflation**. A general decrease in prices is **deflation**. Both have negative effects on the economy. Economic growth occurs when the GDP is constantly growing. A **recession** occurs when there is an absence of growth and the economy shrinks.

The government tries to achieve its economic goals through its **fiscal policy**, or its power to tax and spend money. An increase in government expenditures usually leads to greater economic activity; spending cuts lessen that activity. Tax increases take money out of people's pockets and can slow economic growth. Tax cuts boost economic activity.

(Continues on the next page.)

Lesson Vocabulary

gross domestic product (GDP)   total amount of goods and services produced in a country each year

inflation   general increase in prices throughout the economy

deflation   general decrease in prices throughout the economy

recession   absence of economic growth

fiscal policy   various means the government uses to raise and spend money

TOPIC 12 LESSON 2	**Lesson Summary**
	FISCAL AND MONETARY POLICY (continued)

The Federal Government also uses its **monetary policy**—its ability to control the money supply and the availability of credit in the economy—to regulate the economy. The Fed does this in three ways. It employs **open market operations** to buy or sell government securities, such as bonds, from and to the nation's banks. Buying government securities back from the banks provides money to the banks, which can then make loans to individuals and businesses. Selling securities removes money from banks and the economy. The **reserve requirement** is the amount of money that the Fed requires banks to keep "in reserve" in their vaults or on deposit with one of the twelve Federal Reserve Banks. The **discount rate** is the rate of interest a bank must pay when it borrows money from a Federal Reserve Bank. **Interest** is the cost borrowers incur and must repay in order to borrow money. When the Fed raises the discount rate, banks find it more difficult to obtain money, so they charge higher interest rates to their customers, who then borrow and spend less. Cutting the discount rate has the opposite effect.

While State and local governments can use fiscal policy to affect their economies, they cannot exercise monetary policy, as there is only one central banking system in the United States.

Lesson Vocabulary

monetary policy   process through which the government can influence the nation's economy through changes in the money supply and the availability of credit

open market operations   processes by which the Federal Reserve buys or sells government securities from and to the nation's banks in order to alter the money supply

reserve requirement   amount of money the Federal Reserve determines banks must keep in reserve with one of the Federal Reserve Banks

discount rate   rate of interest a bank must pay when it borrows money from a Federal Reserve Bank

interest   charge for borrowed money, generally a percentage of the amount borrowed

Lesson Summary

FINANCING GOVERNMENT

The Constitution gives the power to tax to Congress, but it places limits on that power. Congress must tax in accord with all parts of the Constitution. It can set taxes for public purposes only and may not tax exports. Direct taxes, except the income tax, must be apportioned according to State population. Indirect tax rates must be the same everywhere. Congress also may not tax any governmental function of a State or its local governments.

Americans today pay several kinds of federal taxes. The largest source of federal revenue, the income tax, is levied on each person's yearly earnings. It is a progressive tax, meaning the higher the income, the higher the tax rate. Each U.S. income-earner files an annual tax return, a form that shows the tax owed. Businesses pay corporate income taxes.

Social insurance taxes fund three programs: 1) the Old-Age, Survivors, and Disability Insurance (OASDI) program, known as Social Security; 2) Medicare, a healthcare program for the elderly; and 3) the unemployment compensation program. These taxes are paid as **payroll taxes**, which employers withhold from paychecks and send to the government. Social insurance taxes are **regressive taxes**, meaning the rate is the same for everyone without regard to income.

Congress places an **excise tax** on the making, selling, and using of certain goods and services, for example, gasoline, tobacco, and alcohol. An **estate tax** must be paid on the assets belonging to a person who has died. An **inheritance tax** is one that is imposed on the portion of an estate inherited by each heir. Gifts from one person to another that are over an annual amount specified by the government are subject to a **gift tax**. Custom duties are taxes laid on goods brought into the United States from another country.

Nontax revenue comes from many sources. A large portion comes from the earnings of the Federal Reserve System, mostly in interest charges. **Interest** is a charge for borrowed money, generally a percentage of the amount borrowed.

Lesson Vocabulary

payroll tax   tax imposed on nearly all employers and their employees, and on self-employed persons, with the amounts owed by employees withheld from their paychecks

regressive tax   tax levied at a flat rate, without regard to the level of a taxpayer's income or ability to pay

excise tax   tax laid on the manufacture, sale, or consumption of goods and/or the performance of services

estate tax   levy imposed on the assets of one who dies

inheritance tax   tax levied on the beneficiary's share of an estate

gift tax   tax on a gift by a living person

interest   charge for borrowing money, generally a percentage of the amount borrowed, which increases regularly until the debt is repaid

MODIFIED CORNELL NOTES

TOPIC **12** LESSON 4	**Lesson Summary**
	SPENDING AND BORROWING

The Federal Government spends huge amounts of money. Most of it is for **entitlements**, or payments made to people whom federal law says are entitled, or have a right, to them. Social Security (Old-Age, Survivors and Disability Insurance, or OASDI) is the largest entitlement program. The next largest areas of expense are national defense and payment on the public debt.

Controllable spending is spending that may be adjusted each year, such as spending on the environment or education. Entitlement spending and payment of the national debt are part of the government's **uncontrollable spending**—payments the government is obliged by law to make each year.

The budget is the Federal Government's spending plan for one year. The President and the Office of Management and Budget put the budget together and then send it to Congress, where it goes to the Budget and Appropriations Committees in each house.

When it has finished reviewing the budget, Congress passes a budget resolution setting spending limits for all federal agencies for the coming year. Congress then passes thirteen appropriations spending bills for the year, each of which the President must sign. If all thirteen bills are not passed before October 1—the beginning of the new fiscal, or budget, year—Congress must pass a **continuing resolution**. Such a bill allows affected agencies to function until new appropriations bills are passed.

The Constitution gives Congress the power to borrow money. For many years, this power was only used to pay the costs of crisis situations, such as wars, or pay for extraordinary large-scale projects. However, for most of the last 80 years, the Federal Government has run up a **deficit**, an amount of money that is less than what was taken in. When the government takes in more than it spends, it

(Continues on the next page.)

Lesson Vocabulary

entitlement   benefit that federal law says must be paid to all those who meet the eligibility requirements, e.g., Medicare, food stamps, and veterans' pension

controllable spending   amount decided upon by Congress and the President to determine how much will be spent each year on many individual government expenditures, including environment protection programs, aid to education, and so on

uncontrollable spending   spending that Congress and the President have no power to change directly

continuing resolution   measure that allows agencies to continue working based on the previous year's appropriations

deficit   yearly shortfall between revenue and spending

MODIFIED CORNELL NOTES

shows a **surplus**. From 1930 to 2013, the annual federal budget has only shown a surplus 13 times.

Prior to the Great Depression, the government had little power to deal with economic crises. After winning the presidency in a landslide victory, Franklin D. Roosevelt and his Democratic government adopted the view advanced by John Maynard Keynes that government should influence the economy by large increases in public spending in times of high unemployment. A key element of Keynesian economics, **demand-side economics** says that if the government borrows to support increased spending, the higher employment that results will produce higher tax revenues. Recent presidents have insisted that lower taxes, not high spending, lead to a stronger economy. This view, which is sometimes called **supply-side economics** or "Reaganomics," is based on the assumption that tax cuts increase the supply of money in private hands and so stimulate the economy.

Congress must authorize all federal borrowing. The actual borrowing is done by the Treasury Department, which issues various kinds of securities to investors. Of course, borrowing produces debt. The annual interest on the federal debt is the amount that must be paid each year to those from whom the government has borrowed. All past deficits that are yet to be repaid, plus interest, add up to form the **public debt**—the total amount of money owed by the government. The debt has often been criticized because it causes concern for the country's future stability.

Lesson Vocabulary

surplus   more income than spending

demand-side economics   theory that the higher employment that results from government borrowing will produce higher tax revenues

supply-side economics   assumption that tax cuts increase the supply of money in private hands and stimulate the economy

public debt   all of the money borrowed by the government and not yet repaid, plus the accrued interest on that money; also called the national debt or federal debt

TOPIC 12 LESSON 5

Lesson Summary
THE UNITED STATES IN THE GLOBAL ECONOMY

There is a growing economic interdependence among nations of the world often called **globalization**. Driven and enabled by advancements in communication and transportation technologies, globalization has also developed out of the drive for increased international trade promoted by the United States. Global trade allows Americans to acquire the goods they want, which this nation cannot produce as cost-effectively or efficiently as it does other goods. Equally important, trade provides Americans with a market for goods and services produced in the U.S., and by doing so it provides Americans with jobs.

Most national governments try to control imports to protect native industries from foreign competition. The goals of this practice, known as **protectionism**, include safeguarding jobs, protecting emerging or weakened industries, and enhancing national security. The government pursues these goals through tariffs, import quotas, and trade embargoes. A **tariff** is a tax on imported goods. It increases the cost of an imported item and makes American-made products more attractive to the domestic customer. An **import quota** is a limit put on the amount of a commodity that can be imported into a country. A **trade embargo** is a ban on trade with a particular country. Together with sanctions, trade embargoes are more often used to apply diplomatic pressure or as a punishment rather than as an economic tool.

The North American Free Trade Agreement, or NAFTA, established free trade among the United States, Canada, and Mexico, and created what amounts to the world's largest free-trade zone. This pact has had positive effects on U.S. trade and investments but has negatively affected some U.S. workers.

The United States plays a great role in influencing international fiscal policy through its leadership in the International Monetary Fund and the World Bank. The International Monetary Fund (IMF)

(Continues on the next page.)

Lesson Vocabulary

globalization   economic interdependence among nations of the world

protectionism   practice of national governments trying to control imports to protect native industries from foreign competition

tariff   tax on imported goods

import quota   limit put on the amount of a commodity that can be imported into a country

trade embargo   ban on trade with a particular country or particular countries

TOPIC 12 LESSON 5

Lesson Summary

THE UNITED STATES IN THE GLOBAL ECONOMY (continued)

aims to structure international trade, create fiscal stability, promote cross-border investment, reduce world poverty, and provide loans to developing nations. The World Bank seeks to reduce world poverty, promote global literacy, and raise the standard of living around the world. The United States also belongs to the World Trade Organization, which provides a set of rules for international commerce, a forum for the creation of new trade agreements, and an arena in which to resolve trade issues. Finally, the United States is a member of the Group of 8, or "G8," an annual meeting of the leaders of eight wealthy and industrialized nations.

For the most part, a global economy is a positive development. More goods are available to consumers and there are more markets in which producers can sell goods. Globalization and international partnerships also help developing nations expand their economies and raise their standards of living by enabling them to sell goods to more affluent countries. And, competition in a global market lowers the price of goods. But, globalization is not without problems. It has led to the exploitation of workers in some less-developed countries, resulted in the United States having large trade deficits with countries such as China, and caused the United States to change from a manufacturing economy to a service economy, in large part because American workers cannot compete with workers in other nations who are paid much less.

TOPIC 12 — Review Questions
GOVERNMENT AND THE ECONOMY

Answer the questions below using the information in the Lesson Summaries on the previous pages.

Lesson 1: Types of Economic Systems

1. Draw Inferences Could any individual take a series of courses on entrepreneurship and become successful? Why or why not?

_____

_____

2. Vocabulary: Use Context Clues What does it mean to nationalize an industry?

_____

_____

Lesson 2: Fiscal and Monetary Policy

3. Summarize Describe how three different governmental institutions carry out the role of the Federal Government in the domestic economy.

_____

_____

4. What is inflation and why would high inflation have a negative effect on the economy?

_____

_____

Lesson 3: Financing Government

5. Draw Inferences What would happen to the government if it did not have the power to tax?

_____

_____

6. Why is the federal income tax considered to be a progressive tax?

_____

_____

Lesson 4: Spending and Borrowing

7. Compare and Contrast What is the difference between controllable and uncontrollable spending?

_____

_____

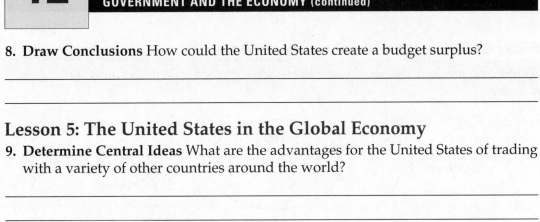

TOPIC
12

Review Questions
GOVERNMENT AND THE ECONOMY (continued)

8. Draw Conclusions How could the United States create a budget surplus?

_____

_____

Lesson 5: The United States in the Global Economy

9. Determine Central Ideas What are the advantages for the United States of trading with a variety of other countries around the world?

_____

_____

10. Identify Causes and Effects How would the World Bank's goals of reducing poverty and raising standards of living around the world be beneficial to the United States in a global economy?

_____

_____

Focus Question: What should governments do?

As you read, note how the states' governments are organized to do the business of the people of the state.

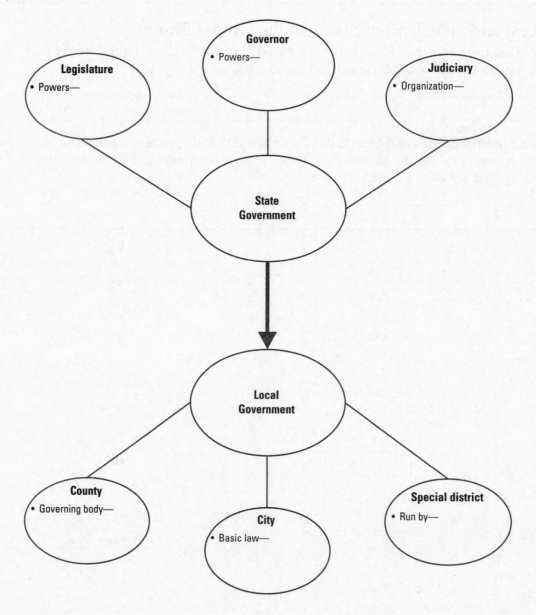

TOPIC 13 LESSON 1 — Lesson Summary
STATE CONSTITUTIONS

Each State has a written constitution, which is that State's supreme law. The first State constitutions were created during or shortly after the Revolution. Each of them proclaimed two major principles: **popular sovereignty**, which means that the people are the sole source of authority for government, and **limited government**, which means that government is given only specific powers. The concepts of separation of powers and checks and balances were also built into the first State constitutions. All current State constitutions include those same provisions. In addition, all current State constitutions include a bill of rights outlining citizens' civil rights, a definition of the structure of State and local governments, and a list detailing the powers of each unit of government.

All State constitutions can be described in terms of six general categories: basic principles, civil rights, governmental structure, governmental powers, processes for change, and miscellaneous provisions.

Constitutional change at the State level has come about through formal amendment. The process involves two basic steps: proposal and ratification by popular vote. While most amendments are proposed by the legislature, in eighteen States, the voters themselves can propose constitutional amendments through the **initiative**—a process in which a certain number of qualified voters sign petitions supporting a proposal. The proposal then goes either to the State legislature or directly on the ballot.

(Continues on the next page.)

Lesson Vocabulary

popular sovereignty   basic principle of the American system of government that asserts that the people are the source of any and all governmental power, and government can exist only with the consent of the governed

limited government   basic principle of American government that states that government is restricted in what it may do, and each individual has rights that government cannot take away

initiative   a process in which a certain number of qualified voters sign petitions in favor of a proposed statute or constitutional amendment, which then goes directly to the ballot

TOPIC 13
LESSON 1

Lesson Summary
STATE CONSTITUTIONS (continued)

Almost all State constitutions are in need of reform because they are out of date. Also, most face the problem of not separating **fundamental law**—those laws of basic and lasting importance, which should be in the constitution—from **statutory law**—laws passed by the legislature.

Lesson Vocabulary

fundamental law   laws of basic and lasting importance that may not easily be changed

statutory law   a law passed by the legislature

TOPIC 13 LESSON 2

Lesson Summary
STATE LEGISLATURES

The legislature is the lawmaking branch of all State governments. It has the power to pass any law that does not conflict with the State constitution or with federal law. All but one of the State legislatures—that of Nebraska—carry out that responsibility as a bicameral body modeled after the U.S. Congress.

Every State's constitution sets out formal requirements of age, citizenship, and residence for legislators. For example, in most States, representatives must be at least twenty-one years old and senators at least twenty-five. In nearly all States, candidates are nominated at party primaries. State legislators serve either two- or four-year terms and are chosen by popular vote. Most State legislatures now hold annual sessions, and several are in session year-round.

All State legislatures are organized much like Congress, with a presiding officer and a committee system. Its members can pass any law that does not conflict with federal law or with any part of the State constitution. Every State legislature's powers include the vital **police power**—the power to protect and promote the public health, safety, morals, and welfare. Each State legislature also possesses nonlegislative powers that enable it to approve appointments, impeach State officers, and exercise **constituent power**—the power to make constitutions and amendments.

The legislative process of the States is also similar to that of Congress. Legislators must introduce bills, but the bills themselves come from a wide range of sources, including interest groups. Several States allow voters to take a direct part in lawmaking. The main vehicles for this participation are the initiative, a process by which voters start and sign petitions to propose a law, and the **referendum**, a process by which a legislative measure is referred to the State's voters for approval.

Lesson Vocabulary

police power the authority of each State to act to protect and promote the public health, safety, morals, and general welfare of its people

constituent power the nonlegislative power of Constitution-making and the constitutional amendment process

referendum a process by which a legislative measure is referred to the State's voters for final approval or rejection

TOPIC 13 LESSON 3 — Lesson Summary
THE GOVERNOR AND STATE ADMINISTRATION

A governor is the chief executive of a State and is popularly elected. In most States, the governor serves a four-year term. Should a vacancy arise in the office, the constitutions of 44 states provide that the lieutenant governor is first in the line of succession. In every state except Oregon, the governor may be removed from office by impeachment and conviction. In 19 States, the governor may be recalled by the voters. The recall is a petition procedure by which voters may remove an elected official from office before the completion of his or her regular term.

The governor is the best-known elected official in the State. However, he or she is not always the most powerful officeholder. In nearly every State, the governor shares power with other executive officers who are also popularly elected. These officials include the lieutenant governor, the secretary of state, the treasurer, and the attorney general.

Like the President the governors of most States have powers of appointment and removal along with supervisory, budget-making, and military powers. The governor also has important legislative and judicial powers. For example, he or she can recommend legislation, call the legislature into special session, and use the **item veto** to veto one or more items in a bill passed by the legislature without having to veto the entire measure.

(Continues on the next page.)

Lesson Vocabulary

item veto   a governor may veto one or more items in a bill without rejecting the entire measure

TOPIC 13 LESSON 3

Lesson Summary
THE GOVERNOR AND STATE ADMINISTRATION (continued)

Most of a governor's judicial powers are powers of executive **clemency**, or mercy that may be shown to those convicted of a crime. For example, by the power to **pardon**, a governor may release a person from being punished for a crime. Through **commutation**, a governor may reduce the sentence imposed by a court. A governor can also grant a **reprieve**, which is a postponement of a sentence. If a governor grants **parole**, he or she sets a prisoner free before the prisoner has finished serving a sentence.

Lesson Vocabulary

clemency   mercy or leniency granted to an offender by a chief executive

pardon   release from punishment or legal consequences of a crime by the President (in a federal case) or a governor (in a State case)

commutation   the power to reduce (commute) the length of a sentence or fine for a crime

reprieve   an official postponement of the execution of a sentence

parole   the release of a prisoner short of the complete term of the original sentence

TOPIC 13 LESSON 4 — Lesson Summary
THE STATE COURTS

The law is the code of conduct governing society. It is made up of several forms of law, including constitutional law, laws based on the U.S. and State constitutions and judicial interpretations of those documents, statutory law, laws enacted by legislatures, and administrative law, laws composed of rules, orders, and regulations issued by executive officers, acting under the authority of constitutional and/or statutory law. Another type of law, **common law**, is the unwritten law that courts have developed over centuries from generally accepted ideas of right and wrong. Once a judge makes a decision in court, it becomes a **precedent**, or a guide to be used in similar cases. Equity, which supplements common law, was developed in England to provide equity—"fairness, justice, and right"—when remedies under the common law fell short of that goal. While common law is mostly remedial, equity is preventative.

The law can also be classified as criminal or civil. **Criminal law** involves cases brought against people accused of committing crimes, which are of two types. A **felony** is the greater crime, punishable by a heavy fine, imprisonment, or death. A **misdemeanor** is a lesser offense, punishable by a small fine or a short jail term. **Civil law** relates to disputes between private parties and between private parties and government. Civil law involves punishment by fines. A tort is a wrongful act that involves injury to one's person, property, or reputation in a situation not covered by the terms of a contract, or legally binding agreement in which one party agrees to do something with or for another party.

A **jury** is a group of people selected to hear evidence and decide questions of fact in a court case. A grand jury is used only in criminal cases. It decides if the State has enough evidence to try someone. For

(Continues on the next page.)

Lesson Vocabulary

common law   an unwritten law made by a judge that has developed over centuries from those generally accepted ideas of right and wrong that have gained judicial recognition

precedent   court decision that stands as an example to be followed in similar cases in the future

criminal law   the portion of the law that defines public wrongs and provides for their punishment

felony   a serious crime that may be punished by a heavy fine and/or imprisonment or even death

misdemeanor   a lesser offense, punishable by a small fine and/or a short jail term

civil law   the portion of the law relating to human conduct, to disputes between private parties, and to disputes between private parties and the government

jury   a body of persons selected according to law who hear evidence and decide questions of fact in a court case

TOPIC 13 LESSON 4

Lesson Summary

THE STATE COURTS (continued)

minor cases, instead of an expensive and time-consuming grand jury many States now use an **information**, which is a formal charge filed by the prosecutor. A petit jury, or trial, jury hears the evidence in a case and decides the disputed facts. Cases in which only minor sums are involved are often heard without a jury, in a bench trial, by the judge alone.

A **justice of the peace**, or JP, presides over justice courts. JPs, who are popularly elected, often try misdemeanors and perform marriages. They may also issue **warrants**, or court orders authorizing an official action, such as an arrest. A JP may also hold a **preliminary hearing**—the first step in a major criminal trial in which the judge decides if enough evidence exists to hold an accused person for action by the grand jury or prosecutor.

Magistrates are the urban equivalent of JPs. They handle minor civil complaints and misdemeanor cases. Municipal courts are organized into divisions, which hear cases of a given kind—for example, civil, criminal, small claims, traffic, and probate divisions.

Most important civil and criminal trials are held in State general trial courts. These general trial courts are courts of "first instance." That is, they exercise original jurisdiction over most of the cases they hear. Individuals under eighteen years of age generally are not subject to the justice of the courts in which adults are tried. Instead, they are tried in juvenile courts.

All but a few States have one or more intermediate appellate courts, or courts of appeals. These courts mostly exercise **appellate jurisdiction**; they have the authority to review the rulings of lower courts. The State supreme court is the court of last resort in a State's judicial system. It has the final say in all matters of State law.

The governor appoints justices in half the States. In most other States, popular election is the method for selecting judges. Finding the best method has inspired much debate.

Lesson Vocabulary

information   a formal charge filed by a prosecutor without the action of a grand jury

justice of the peace   a judge who stands on the lowest level of the State judicial system and presides over justice courts

warrant   a court order authorizing, or making legal, some official action such as a search or an arrest

preliminary hearing   the first step in a major criminal prosecution where the judge decides if the evidence is enough to hold the person for action by the grand jury or the prosecutor

appellate jurisdiction   the authority of a court to review decisions of inferior (lower) courts

TOPIC 13 LESSON 5

Lesson Summary
LOCAL GOVERNMENTS – STRUCTURE AND FUNCTION

The State creates and authorizes all local governments, which can take multiple forms. A **county** is the major unit of local government in most States. Counties are often divided into **townships**, which share the functions of rural local government with the counties. In some States, towns carry out most of the functions performed elsewhere by counties.

A county typically has four major elements: a governing body, a number of boards or commissions, appointed bureaucrats, and a variety of elected officials. The county's governing body is frequently called the county board. Generally, county boards can be grouped into two types: boards of commissioners and boards of supervisors. The board of commissioners is the smaller, more common type. The State constitution and acts of the State legislature spell out the powers held by county governing bodies. Those powers are usually both executive and legislative. Historically, nearly all counties have been institutions of rural government and they remain so today.

Tribal governments exist as a distinct form of government. Unlike State, county, or community governments, the governments of recognized Native American nations have the right to govern their own people on their own territories unless otherwise specified by treaty acts of Congress. Typically, a tribal government has an elected leader called a chief or chairperson and a council, which can vary in size. Tribal governments vary widely in size and structure and the services they provide.

Towns and townships exist in nearly half the States. In New England, the town is a major unit of local government. A town generally includes rural and urban areas. It delivers services provided elsewhere by cities and counties. A board of selectmen/selectwomen manages town business between annual town meetings, at which voters decide the town's taxes, spending, and other concerns.

Townships are found as units of local government in other parts of the country. About half of them provide for annual township meetings, like those held in New England towns. Otherwise, the governing body is a three- or five-member board, generally called the board of trustees or board of supervisors. A municipality is an urban political unit within a township that usually exists as a separate governmental entity. As a result, township functions tend to be rural.

There are thousands of special districts across the country. A **special district** performs governmental functions at the local level and is usually

(Continues on the next page.)

Lesson Vocabulary

county   a major unit of local government in most States

township   a subdivision of a county

special district   an independent unit created to perform one or more related governmental functions at the local level

MODIFIED CORNELL NOTES

run by an elected board. Examples are school districts and districts that provide water, police protection, and bridge and park maintenance.

During its history the United States has shifted from a primarily rural population to a primarily urban one. When large numbers of people live close to one another, there is more demand on local governments to provide water, police and fire protection, sewer management, waste removal, traffic regulation, public health facilities, schools, and recreation. Depending on local custom and State law, municipalities may be known as cities, towns, boroughs, or villages. The larger municipalities are known everywhere as cities, and the usual practice is to use that title only for those communities with significant populations. The process by which a State establishes a city as a legal body is called incorporation.

A city's basic law, or its constitution, is its **charter**. The **mayor-council government** is the oldest and most widely used type of city government. In a **strong-mayor government**, the mayor heads the city's administration, hires and fires employees, and prepares the budget. In a **weak-mayor government**, the mayor shares executive duties with other elected officials and the city council. In a **commission government**, three to nine popularly elected commissioners form a city council. Each also heads a department of city government. A **council-manager government** features a strong council of five to seven members elected on a nonpartisan ballot, a weak mayor, and a city manager named by the council.

(Continues on the next page.)

Lesson Vocabulary

charter   a city's basic law, its constitution; a written grant of authority from the king

mayor-council government   the oldest and most widely used type of city government, which includes an elected mayor as the chief executive and an elected council as its legislative body

strong-mayor government   a type of government in which the mayor heads the city's administration

weak-mayor government   a type of government in which the mayor shares his or her executive duties with other elected officials

commission government   a government formed by commissioners, heads of different departments of city government, who are popularly elected to form the city council, thus incorporating both legislative and executive powers in one body

council-manager government   a modification of the mayor-council government, it consists of a strong council of members elected on a non-partisan ballot, a weak mayor who is elected by the people, and a manager who is named by the council

TOPIC 13 LESSON 5	**Lesson Summary**
	LOCAL GOVERNMENTS – STRUCTURE AND FUNCTION (continued)

MODIFIED CORNELL NOTES

While many American cities developed haphazardly, **zoning**, the practice of dividing a city into districts and regulating the uses of property in each district is now used, to ensure orderly growth. In this form of city planning, land is generally placed in one of three zones—residential, commercial, or industrial.

Today, about half of all Americans live in suburbs. The movement of people out of cities deprives cities of many civic, financial, and social resources. Attempts to meet the needs of **metropolitan areas**—cities and the areas around them—have included the annexation of outlying areas and the creation of special districts set up for a single purpose, such as parks.

Lesson Vocabulary

zoning   the practice of dividing a city into a number of districts and regulating the uses of that property

metropolitan area   a city and the area around it

TOPIC 13 LESSON 6

Lesson Summary
STATE AND LOCAL SPENDING AND REVENUE

The 50 States provide many services to their citizens. They do so directly through State agencies and programs and indirectly through local governments.

Education is one of the most important—and expensive—responsibilities of the States. Local governments fund primary and secondary education, with some help from the State's government. The States also administer public university systems.

The States work to promote the welfare of their citizens through many means. For example, they fund public health programs such as Medicaid, which gives low-income families medical insurance. They also contribute to **welfare**—cash assistance to the poor. This is an **entitlement** program—one in which anyone who meets the eligibility requirements is entitled to receive benefits. The State promotes public welfare in many other ways, including enforcing antipollution laws and protecting worker safety.

The States protect public safety by providing police units and correctional facilities for people convicted of State crimes. State criminal corrections spending has greatly increased because of increased numbers of convicts and lengths of prison terms.

Each State builds and maintains all highways and roads within its boundaries. The State receives federal funds to assist with interstate highway maintenance; however, building and maintaining the roads and highways is an enormous job. It regularly ranks high in the State budget.

State and local governments collect taxes to pay for the many services they provide. The U.S. Constitution, the Fourteenth Amendment, and State constitutions limit taxing. State legislatures decide what taxes the State and localities will levy and at what rates.

(Continues on the next page.)

Lesson Vocabulary

welfare   cash assistance to the poor

entitlement   a benefit that federal law says must be paid to all those who meet the eligibility requirements, e.g., Medicare, food stamps, and veterans' pension

MODIFIED CORNELL NOTES

In most States, the largest source of revenue is State taxes. Another significant source of revenue is the **sales tax**, which is a tax placed on the sale of various commodities; the purchaser pays it. Sales tax is a **regressive tax**—one that does not vary according to a person's ability to pay.

An **income tax** is collected on the earnings of individuals and corporations. Individual income tax is usually a **progressive tax**—that is, the higher your income, the more tax you pay. Corporate income tax rates are usually a fixed percentage of income. Of the 50 States, 43 States levy and collect a personal income and 46 have a corporate income tax.

The largest source of income for local governments is the **property tax**—a levy on real property, such as land, or personal property, which includes bank accounts. The process of determining the value of the property to be taxed is called **assessment**. Heirs pay an **inheritance tax** on their shares of an estate. An **estate tax** is levied directly on the full estate itself.

Other sources of State and local revenues include license taxes, document transfer taxes, and amusement taxes. State and local governments also receive nontax revenue through federal grants and publicly operated enterprises such as toll roads or lotteries. A **State budget** is a financial plan for the use of public money, personnel, and property. Today 47 States have adopted the executive budget, which gives the governor two vital powers: (1) to prepare the State's budget, and, after the legislature has acted upon his or her recommendations, (2) to manage the spending of the monies set aside by the legislature. The basic steps in the budget process are much the same at the State, local, and federal levels.

Lesson Vocabulary

sales tax   a tax placed on the sale of various commodities, paid by the purchaser

regressive tax   a tax levied at a flat rate, without regard to the level of a taxpayer's income or ability to pay

income tax   a tax levied on the income of individuals and/or corporations

progressive tax   a type of tax proportionate to income

property tax   a tax levied on real and personal property

assessment   the process of determining the value of property to be taxed

inheritance tax   a tax levied on the beneficiary's share of an estate

estate tax   a levy imposed on the assets of one who dies

state budget   a State's financial plan for the use of public money, personnel, and property

Answer the questions below using the information in the Lesson Summaries on the previous pages.

Lesson 1: State Constitutions

1. What document serves as supreme law in each state?

_____

_____

2. What are the two main steps involved in revising or amending a State constitution?

_____

_____

Lesson 2: State Legislatures

3. Draw Conclusions Why do you think the State legislatures are modeled on the Congress?

_____

_____

4. Compare and Contrast How does an initiative differ from a referendum?

_____

_____

Lesson 3: The Governor and State Administration

5. What important legislative powers do governors possess?

_____

_____

6. What happens when a governor grants parole?

_____

_____

Lesson 4: The State Courts

7. Compare and Contrast What is the difference between criminal law and civil law? Provide an example for each in your answer.

_____

_____

8. Draw Inferences Which level of a state's courts would most likely hear a case involving a person speeding through a school zone?

_____

_____

Lesson 5: Local Governments – Structure and Function

9. Why are special districts created?

_____

_____

10. Compare and Contrast What is the biggest difference between the mayor-council form of government and the commission form?

_____

_____

Lesson 6: State and Local Spending and Revenue

11. Identify Main Ideas How is public education funded?

_____

_____

12. Compare and Contrast What is the difference between a regressive tax and a progressive tax? Give one example of each.

_____

_____

TOPIC 14 Note Taking Study Guide
COMPARATIVE POLITICAL SYSTEMS

Focus Question: What makes a government successful?

As you read, note details about each government and consider the role that its governing institutions play in its success.

Comparative Political Systems

Country	Form of Government	Governing Power
United Kingdom		Executive— Legislative— Judicial—
Russian Federation		Executive— Legislative— Judicial—
China		Executive— Legislative— Judicial—

MODIFIED CORNELL NOTES

Democratization refers to the change from dictatorship to democracy and is marked by the holding of free and fair elections. Internal and external pressure for democratization may pit ruling **hard-liners**, who often blame foreign enemies or internal critics for undermining the state, against ruling **reformers**, who may recognize the need to relinquish some power, even if not to fully give up power or to democratize. That is why the apparently small step of recognizing an opposition leader or party is actually a significant step toward democracy.

The dramatic fall of the Soviet Union to the democratic demands of citizens shows that the process of democratic transition is not automatic. Democracy requires that established governing institutions, such as the military and police force, give up power, which can disrupt the social order people expect government to provide. Significant economic problems also can devastate the public's view of democracy itself.

As the ultimate positive outcome of democratization, **democratic consolidation** occurs when a country firmly establishes the necessary factors for vibrant democracy and social order. These factors include a free press, a competitive group of political parties, a civilian-controlled military and security force, and a number of engaged interest groups. Additionally, an economic system that rewards innovation and hard work, and a professional civil service implementing governing decisions are needed. Most of all, democratic consolidation occurs when a society establishes a sense of common trust among its citizens. Trust is vital because democracy requires that losers of elections accept the outcomes instead of trying to undermine their opponents' newly won democratic institutions.

Young countries such as Somalia that fail to develop the needed factors for democratic success are known as **failed states**. In most of

(Continues on the next page.)

Lesson Vocabulary

democratization   the change from dictatorship to democracy, marked by the holding of free and fair elections

hard-liners   those who fight to maintain the status quo

reformers   those who work to change or reform government

democratic consolidation   the process of establishing the factors considered necessary for a democracy to succeed

failed states   nations in which security is nonexistent, the economy has collapsed, healthcare and school systems are in shambles, and corruption is flourishing

TOPIC 14 LESSON 1 — Lesson Summary
DEMOCRACY AND THE CHANGING WORLD (continued)

these areas, security is nonexistent, the economy has collapsed, the healthcare and school systems are in shambles, and corruption flourishes. **State-building** efforts by outside countries attempt to strengthen the governing institutions of a country and lead to the country's stability and democratization.

Lesson Vocabulary

state-building   the process where outside countries attempt to strengthen the governing institutions of a country

MODIFIED CORNELL NOTES

The United Kingdom, which consists of England, Scotland, Wales, and Northern Ireland, is a democracy with a unitary, parliamentary government. Its constitution consists of written documents and unwritten customs and practices.

The United Kingdom's government is a monarchy, but today the monarch, or queen, is a figurehead who reigns but does not rule. The prime minister holds the real power of government. Like the United States, the United Kingdom is an example of **constitutionalism**, government in which power is distributed and limited by a system of laws that must be obeyed by its rulers.

The United Kingdom is a **parliamentary system**, where the chief executive—the prime minister—is chosen by the parliament rather than being directly elected. The United Kingdom's bicameral Parliament holds the nation's legislative and executive powers. The lower house is the House of Commons. Its 650 members of Parliament, or MPs, are popularly elected. Members of the House of Commons tend to have little influence on legislation, and their votes are almost always bound by party loyalty. A general election of every seat in the Commons occurs at least every five years. Its upper house is the House of Lords, whose members have either inherited their seats—a practice that ended in 1999—or been appointed for life. The House of Lords has limited power.

The prime minister is the leader of the party that holds a majority in the Commons. If no party holds a majority, a temporary alliance of parties, or a **coalition**, chooses a prime minister. The prime minister selects the cabinet members, or **ministers**, who head the executive departments. Each opposition party appoints its own team of potential cabinet members, called the **shadow cabinet,** in case it gains power.

(Continues on the next page.)

Lesson Vocabulary

constitutionalism   basic principle that government and those who govern must obey the law; the rule of law

parliamentary system   a form of government in which the executive branch is made up of the prime minister, or premier, and that official's cabinet

coalition   a temporary alliance of several groups who come together to form a working majority to control a government

ministers   cabinet members, most commonly of the House of Commons

shadow cabinet   members of opposition parties who watch, or shadow, particular cabinet members and would be ready to run the government

The court system decides cases based on **common law**, where laws are adjudicated according to judicial precedent. Because there is no singular constitution, weighing decisions based on previous court decisions is vital for British democratic consistency.

The United Kingdom recently began a process of **devolution**, or delegating authority to regional governments. This is intended to provide for the distinct governmental needs of the United Kingdom's four nations.

Seating in the House of Commons suggests how policy is made. The prime minister and cabinet ministers sit in the front bench across from the shadow cabinet of the main opposition party. Fellow party members sit on benches behind the government or shadow cabinet and are referred to as **backbenchers**, who have little or no influence over policy. Government in the United Kingdom is referred to as a **party government**, where a winning party creates and carries out policy with overwhelming party loyalty based on the party's platform.

The United States and the United Kingdom have similar common law judicial systems that rely on precedent from earlier decisions to guide a judge's decisions. Constitutionalism, the rule of law, and recognition of citizens' rights play a large part in both democracies. However, the United States is a federal system with some areas of policy reserved to States, while the United Kingdom is a unitary system with Parliament having sovereignty. The United Kingdom is a parliamentary system where parliament chooses the prime minister rather than the chief executive being publicly elected like the American President. Lastly, British government is a party government while the United States is not.

Lesson Vocabulary

common law a body of unwritten law made by judges' rulings that has developed over centuries from those generally accepted ideas of right and wrong that have gained judicial recognition

devolution the delegation of authority from the central government to regional governments

backbencher a member of the House of Commons who is not a party leader

party government the direction and control of the processes of government by the party who has majority favor

Name _____ Class _____ Date _____

MODIFIED CORNELL NOTES

The Soviet Union used to be the largest country in the world. It was the modern successor to the Russian empire, which ended in 1917 when a revolution overthrew the emperor, or czar. In the same year, Vladimir Lenin led another revolution, which brought the Communist Party to power and established the Soviet Union. After Lenin's death in 1924, Josef Stalin became the new Soviet leader. He consolidated his power with **purges**, in which he jailed, exiled, and executed opponents. He also built the Soviet Union into a major military and industrial power.

The Soviet Union's official name was the Union of Soviet Socialist Republics (USSR). It was composed of 15 republics, among which Russia was dominant. The Communist Party leaders made all major decisions.

In 1985, Mikhail Gorbachev began a reform program based on two principles. *Perestroika* was the restructuring of economic and political life. *Glasnost* was the policy of openness under which the government increased its tolerance of dissent and freedom of expression. A wave of democratization led to the Soviet Union's complete collapse in 1992.

The Russian government is now struggling toward democracy and economic reform. It has a multi-party system. The popularly elected president has great power, although the government does have executive, legislative, and judicial branches. The president appoints a prime minister who is second-in-command. The bicameral legislature is called the Federal Assembly; it is composed of the Council of the Federation and the State Duma, which is the more powerful chamber. The elected members of the Constitutional Court have the power of judicial review.

The constitutional powers and practices of Russia's presidents have given them considerable power to set policy by decree. Unlike in the United States, Russian presidents can order the government to carry out a policy of the president's choice, and the legislature must pass legislation in order to negate the decree.

The United States and Russia are both international powers and federal democracies with far-flung and diverse regional governments. Both governments have separately elected presidents (though the Russian system includes a prime minister) and bicameral legislatures. However, Russian presidents have more power than do American presidents. Because Russians prefer strong leaders and will vote them in with a mandate to govern, other actors like interest groups and the media that significantly affect American politics lack major influence in Russia.

Lesson Vocabulary

purge   a process of government purification by removing rivals

TOPIC 14 LESSON 4 — Lesson Summary
CHINA

In 1949, communist leader Mao Zedong took over China and established the People's Republic of China. In the mid-1960s, Mao tried to destroy China's "old" ways with the Cultural Revolution. Beginning in 1966, Mao's young Red Guards attacked teachers, intellectuals, and anyone else who seemed to lack enthusiasm for the revolution. By 1968, however, the Cultural Revolution had caused such chaos that Mao halted it.

China's Communist Party is the country's government. Top members of the party hold the highest positions in the government and the military. They encourage economic reforms but impose harsh limits on human rights.

China's national government has two main bodies: the National People's Congress and the State Council. The deputies of the National People's Congress are elected to five-year terms. According to the Chinese constitution, the Congress is the highest governmental **authority**, but in reality it has little power. The State Council is the main body in the executive branch of government. Its head is the premier, who is chosen by the Central Committee of the Communist Party.

A nationwide system of "people's courts" deals with both civil and criminal cases. These courts are supervised by the Supreme People's Court.

China's central government exerts direct control over local political subdivisions, which include 22 provinces and 5 autonomous—independent—regions inhabited by ethnic minorities. Tensions continue between the People's Republic of China and Taiwan over which represents the official Chinese government.

There are very few comparisons to draw between American politics and Chinese politics. American politics tends to be decentralized, full of checks and balances, and influenced by multiple actors, such as interest groups, the media, and public opinion. China, on the other hand, is completely governed by a single party, and more specifically by the top level of that party. There are no formal mechanisms to affect governance or policy. Ironically, both countries govern themselves differently but have become increasingly linked internationally.

Lesson Vocabulary

authority   the power or right to direct or control someone or something

TOPIC 14 Review Questions
COMPARATIVE POLITICAL SYSTEMS

Answer the questions below using the information in the Lesson Summaries on the previous pages.

Lesson 1: Democracy and the Changing World

1. Draw Conclusions Why is a country's holding of its first free and fair elections such a vital step in the process of democratization?

_____

_____

2. Identify Key Steps in a Process How might the United States help other countries build strong, independent democratic institutions?

_____

_____

Lesson 2: The United Kingdom

3. How would you describe the United Kingdom's constitution?

_____

_____

4. Compare and Contrast What is the difference between the American federal system of government and the United Kingdom's unitary system of government?

_____

_____

Lesson 3: The Russian Federation

5. What are some powers that the Russian president has that the President of the United States does not have?

_____

_____

6. Draw Inferences Do you think Russia is moving steadily toward democratic consolidation? Why or why not?

_____

_____

Lesson 4: China

7. Identify Main Ideas Complete this sentence: China's government is completely controlled by _____.

_____

_____

8. Determine Central Ideas The Chinese Communist Party has 82 million members, which only translates to about 6 percent of the Chinese public. How do you think the Communist Party is able to stay in power?

_____

_____